HOW IT WORKS

WEATHER

MICHAEL ALLABY

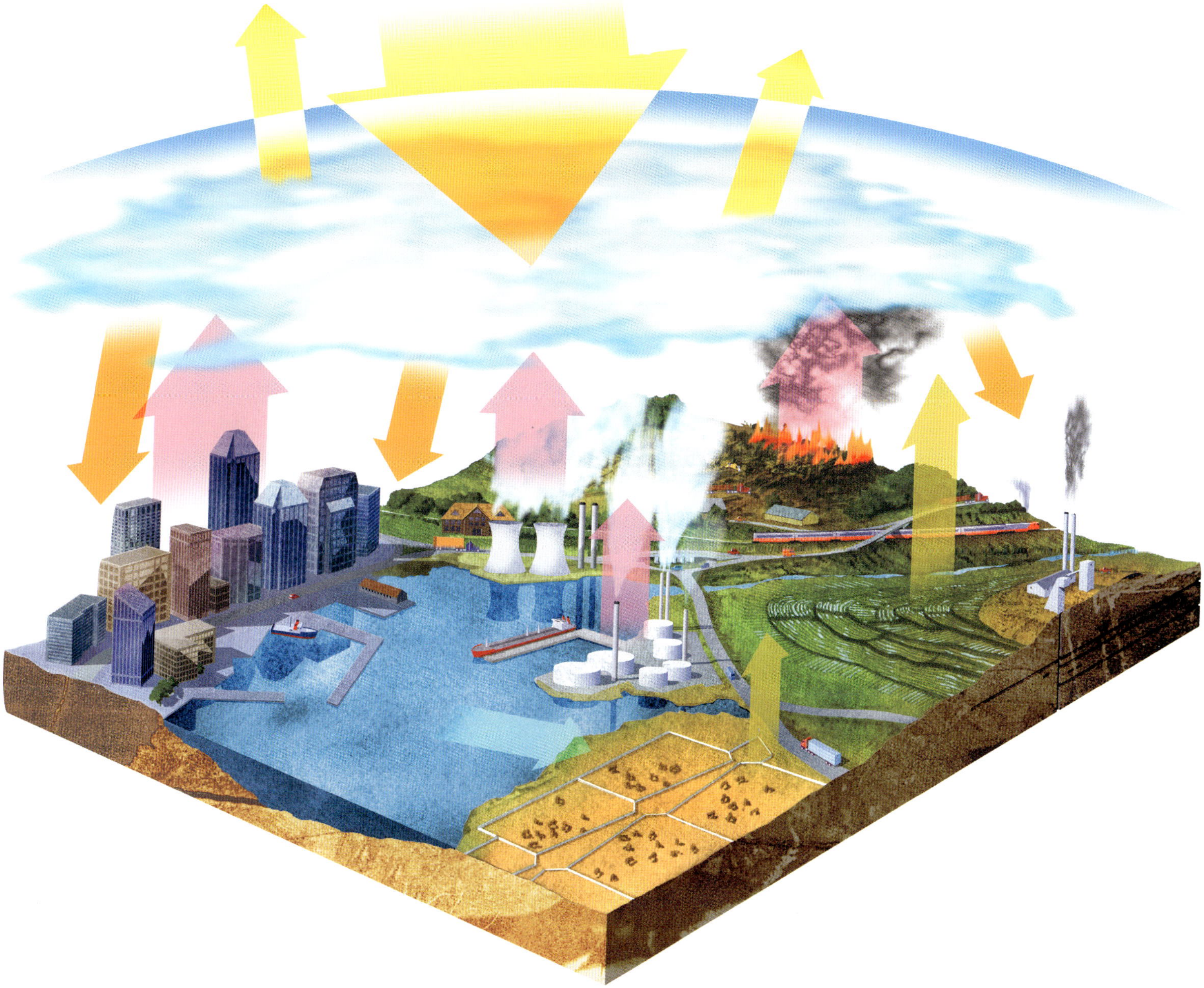

award

Series editor: Elizabeth Miles
Cover design: Duck Egg Blue
Illustrations: David Draper, Martin Sanders,
Mike Saunders, Jim Channell

Photography and additional illustrations: Shutterstock.com (Aaron Kelly79, ajt, Akimov Igor, aleksandr shepitko, andreonegin, Bogdan Wankowicz, Borislav Bajkic, Brisbane, Darryl Brooks, DarkOne, Daniel Rajszczak, David Steele, Digoarpi, Dollatum Hanrud, Dustie, Edward Haylan, elRoce, EmiliaUngur, fokke baarssen, glen gaffney, Hung Chung Chih, Iman.Ebrahimi, Jeff Smith - Perspectives, Jerome Scholler, Le Do, lunamarina, Madlen, Marek CECH, Melanie Metz, Menno van der Haven, Mikado767, Mike Richter, Minerva Studio, NASA Earth Observation Images, Olivier Le Queinec, PhilipYb Studio, Phonlamai Photo, Picture Partners, Piotr Krzeslak, Pushish Images, Robert Adrian Hillman, titoOnz, Todd Shoemake, Tony Rix, YONGYUT.TT, Yulia Emelianenko, Yury Kosourov), ESA, NASA

ISBN 978-1-78270-009-8

Copyright © Award Publications Limited

All rights reserved. No part of this publication may be reproduced or utilised in any form or by any means electronic or mechanical, including photocopying, recording, or by any information storage and retrieval system now known or hereafter invented, without the prior written permission of the publisher.

This edition first published 2025

Published by Award Publications Limited,
The Old Riding School, Welbeck,
Worksop, S80 3LR

/awardpublications @award.books
www.awardpublications.co.uk

23-1100 1

Printed in China

Contents

The Sun's Power	6	Wind and Water	28
Climate	8	Measuring	30
Wind Machine	10	Satellites	32
Water World	12	Forecasts	34
Clouds	14	Pollution	36
Highs and Lows	16	Changing Climate	38
Fronts	18	Protection	40
Rain and Snow	20	Renewable Energy	42
Thunderstorms	22	Landscapes	44
Hurricanes	24	Index	46
Tornadoes	26		

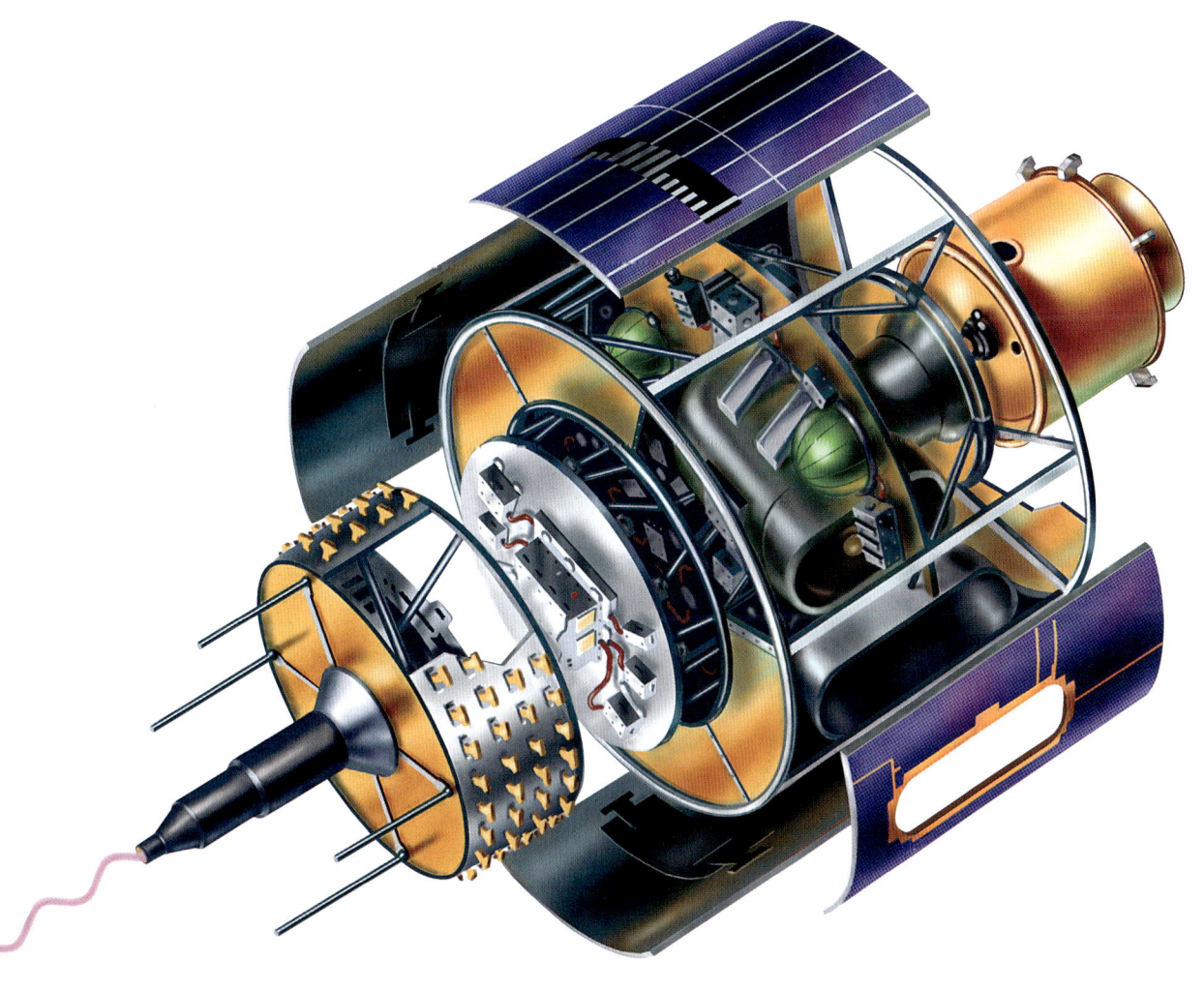

The Sun's Power

The Sun is a star. Like other stars, it is a huge nuclear furnace that gives off the light that we see by and heat that we can feel. If the Sun were not there, the Earth would be a bitterly cold, dark, dead place.

The Earth is surrounded by the atmosphere, a blanket of different layers of gases. We call this mixture of gases 'air'. Some of the radiation (energy) that reaches Earth from the Sun is absorbed near the top of the atmosphere, but most passes through the air all the way to the surface of the land and sea. Some is reflected by bright clouds, snow and other light-coloured objects. The rest is absorbed, warming the ground and the water. When land and sea are warmed, they, in turn, warm the air next to them. The warm air rises, and this movement of air causes the weather.

Trapped

The Sun emits particles. Some are captured by the Earth's magnetic field. They are swept down and around the North and South Poles. They give off light when they collide with atoms of oxygen and nitrogen in the air. This creates the Northern and Southern Lights, or aurorae. Like curtains of light, they ripple more than 300 kilometres above our heads.

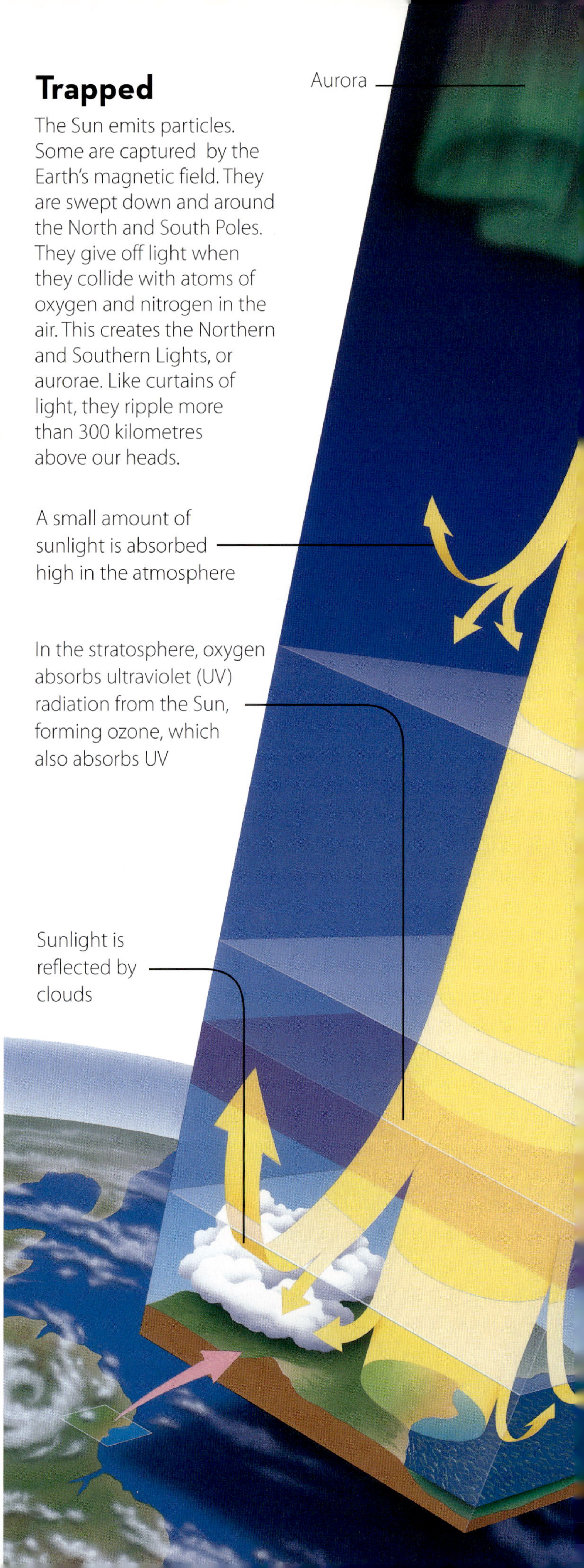

Aurora

A small amount of sunlight is absorbed high in the atmosphere

In the stratosphere, oxygen absorbs ultraviolet (UV) radiation from the Sun, forming ozone, which also absorbs UV

Sunlight is reflected by clouds

Reflected light

All surfaces reflect some of the sunlight falling on them. Bare soil exposed when forest trees are cut down (**1**) reflects about 25 per cent. A forest (**2**) reflects about 15 per cent. Conifer (pine) forests reflect less than broad-leaved forests because they are darker. A field of wheat (**3**) reflects about 20 per cent, while fresh snow on a mountainside reflects about 90 per cent (**4**).

There is no clearly defined top to the atmosphere; the air just gets thinner and thinner

The four seasons

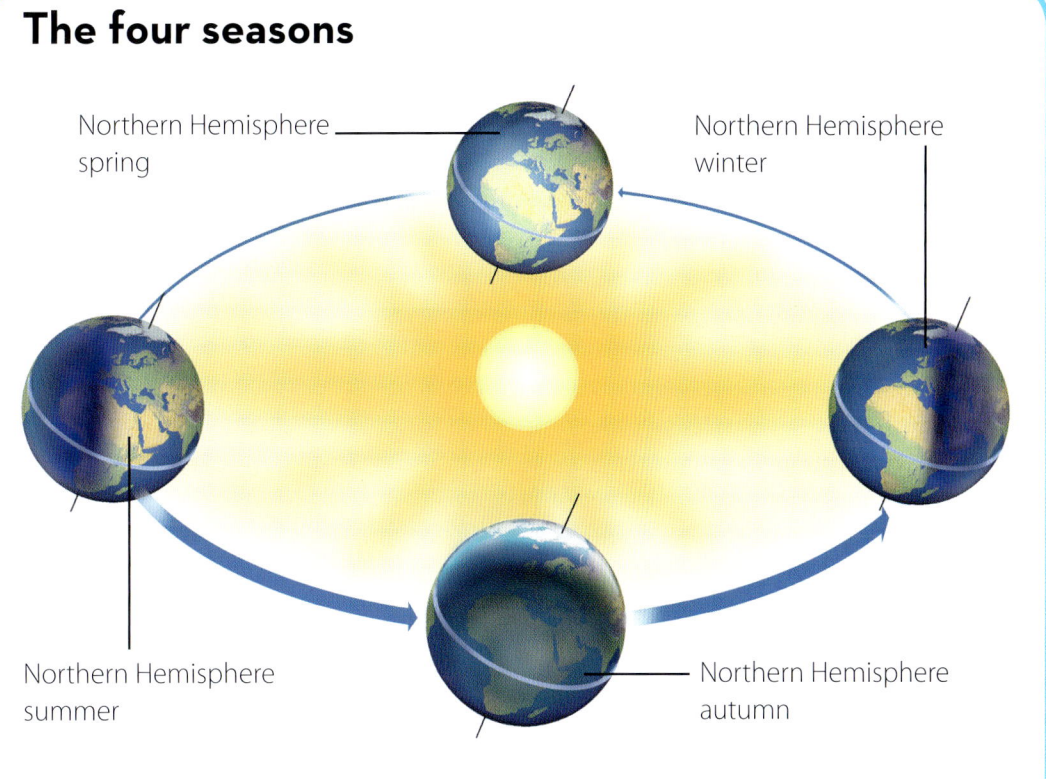

Northern Hemisphere spring

Northern Hemisphere winter

Northern Hemisphere summer

Northern Hemisphere autumn

The Earth spins on its axis, but the axis is not vertical. This means that as the Earth moves around the Sun, first one half is tilted towards the Sun, and then the other. It is summer in the half facing the Sun and winter in the other half. In spring and autumn the Sun shines on both halves equally.

The mesosphere ends at about 80 kilometres above the Earth's surface

The boundary at the bottom of the mesosphere is called the stratopause

Ozone is concentrated in the ozone layer – it helps to protect us from the Sun's UV rays

The ground also radiates warmth into the air

We inhabit the troposphere

Atmosphere

The atmosphere extends to about 1,000 kilometres above the Earth, but 99.9 per cent of the air is in the lowest 50 kilometres. Above about 6 kilometres there is not enough air to breathe. As you climb, the temperature falls. It goes on falling until about 12 kilometres, where it is about −60 °C, then it remains the same. This height marks the boundary, called the tropopause, between the troposphere below and the stratosphere above. Weather happens in the troposphere. Above about 20 kilometres the temperature starts to rise again. This is because oxygen is absorbing ultraviolet (UV) radiation from the Sun and forming ozone. The absorption of this radiation heats the air.

The stratosphere ends at the stratopause, about 50 kilometres above the Earth's surface. Beyond that lies the mesosphere, where the temperature decreases again. It ends at the mesopause, at about 80 kilometres. Above the mesopause, the thermosphere merges gradually with space.

Climate

The prairies of North America (1) and steppes of Eurasia (2) are vast grassland areas. Go to the centre of Brazil (3) and you will find the land covered with tropical rainforest. Most of North Africa (4) and the Arabian Peninsula (5) is desert. The plants and animals that live in each of these areas, or biomes, are very different, but each is typical of the climate that affects the area.

Climate is the pattern of weather recorded at a place over a long period of time. Every part of the world has its own climate. Each climate is associated with certain kinds of plants and the animals that live among those plants. Climates are often classified according to the type of vegetation or farming they support.

Continental grasslands

Bison have thick coats that keep them warm in the bitterly cold winters on the North American prairie. The grasses of the prairies, the South American Pampas and Eurasian Steppe grow well in dry continental climates.

Tropical forest

Tropical forests grow where the weather is always warm. Some places have rain all year; in others it is seasonal.

Desert

It seldom rains in a desert. Many deserts are hot, but not all of them. Some deserts in Central Asia and Argentina are a result of their cold climate.

Temperate

These regions are rarely very hot or cold. Rainfall is moderate – in some places seasonal, while in others it falls all year round.

Continents

On large land masses, or continents, the climate is fairly dry far from the ocean. Summers are often very hot and winters very cold.

Polar

Temperatures are below freezing most or all of the year. In Antarctica and central Greenland the weather is very dry.

Highland

Temperature decreases with altitude. This means a mountain climate can be tropical at the base and polar at the summit.

8

Polar climate

Polar bears spend much of their time on the Arctic ice that surrounds the North Pole. They have thick coats and fur on the soles of their feet. Tundra vegetation (grasses, sedges, rushes and small bushes) grows around the edge of the Arctic.

Temperate climate

The mild winters, warm summers and rain throughout the year, plus dry, sunny spells to ripen grain, create a temperate climate – ideal for growing crops and raising cattle on pasture.

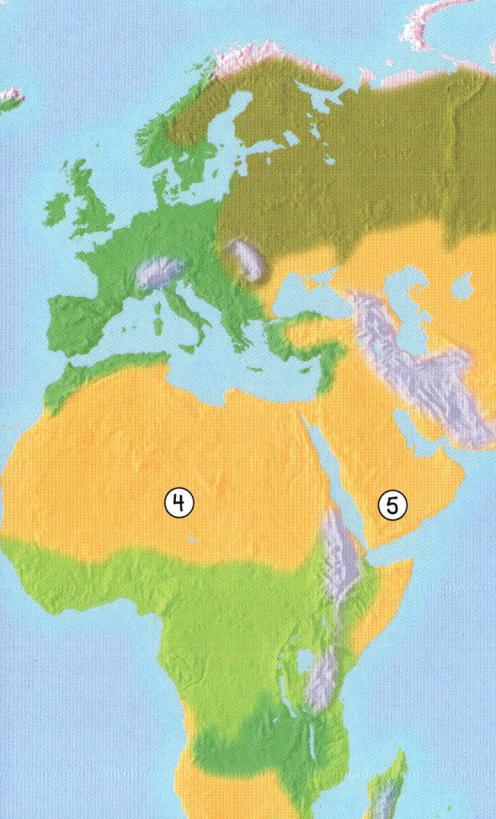

Highland

Many mountain plants and animals live at only one level, but deer, sheep and goats feed on high pastures in summer and move lower down in winter. The agile mountain lion, or puma, follows them.

Desert

The dromedary camel thrives in the dry, hot desert. Its body does not overheat and it can survive for up to two weeks without food or water.

Tropical forest

Constant warmth and lots of rain produce the giant trees and other plants of the tropical rainforests. There is plenty to eat for tree-dwellers such as South American spider monkeys.

Wind Machine

Wind is moving air. Air moves because there is less of it in some places than in others. When air is warm it expands. Its molecules move further apart, so they occupy more space and the air becomes less dense. Cold air is denser. Its molecules crowd closer together, so there are more of them in any given space. Air flows from where it is dense to where the molecules are less crowded – a little like air rushing out of a bike tyre when you remove the valve.

If the Sun heated the Earth evenly, and the land and sea were warmed and cooled equally everywhere, there would be no wind. But this is not what happens. Some places are warmer than others and so air is denser in some places. Winds help distribute the Sun's warmth. They carry warm air into cold places and cold air into warm places.

Trade winds

Trade winds are the most reliable winds on Earth. They blow towards the Equator, from the northeast in the Northern Hemisphere and from the southeast in the Southern Hemisphere. Where they meet, the air rises and huge rain clouds form. The air descends again and flows back towards the Equator, and so produces the trade winds.

One of two jet streams in the Northern Hemisphere

Parts of the global wind system flow in circular patterns called cells; this is the mid-latitude Ferrel cell

Dry, warm air sinks

Warm, moist air rises, then moves away from the Equator

The Equator divides the globe

The Earth rotates from west to east, making the winds curve

This vertical movement of tropical air is called a Hadley cell

Cold, dense air sinks over the poles, then flows away from the polar regions

Cold air flowing south meets warm air flowing north, and the air rises

Air rises in the Ferrel cell where cold, polar air meets warmer air from the middle latitudes

The Sun's rays

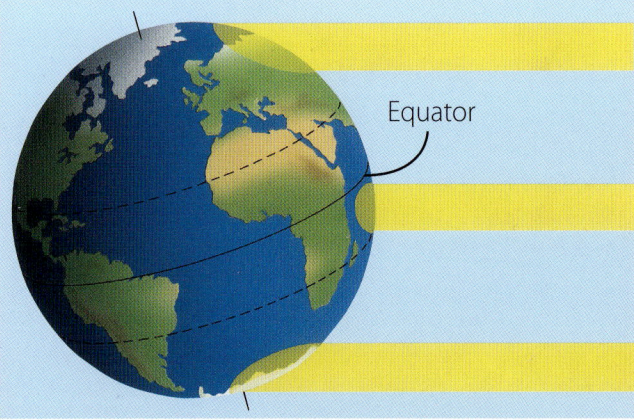

Near the Equator the Sun is almost directly overhead at noon. It shines very intensely because its rays are concentrated. Near the Arctic and Antarctica the Sun is low in the sky, even in summer. Its rays are less intense because they are spread over a wider area. That is why it is warmer at the Equator than near the North and South Poles.

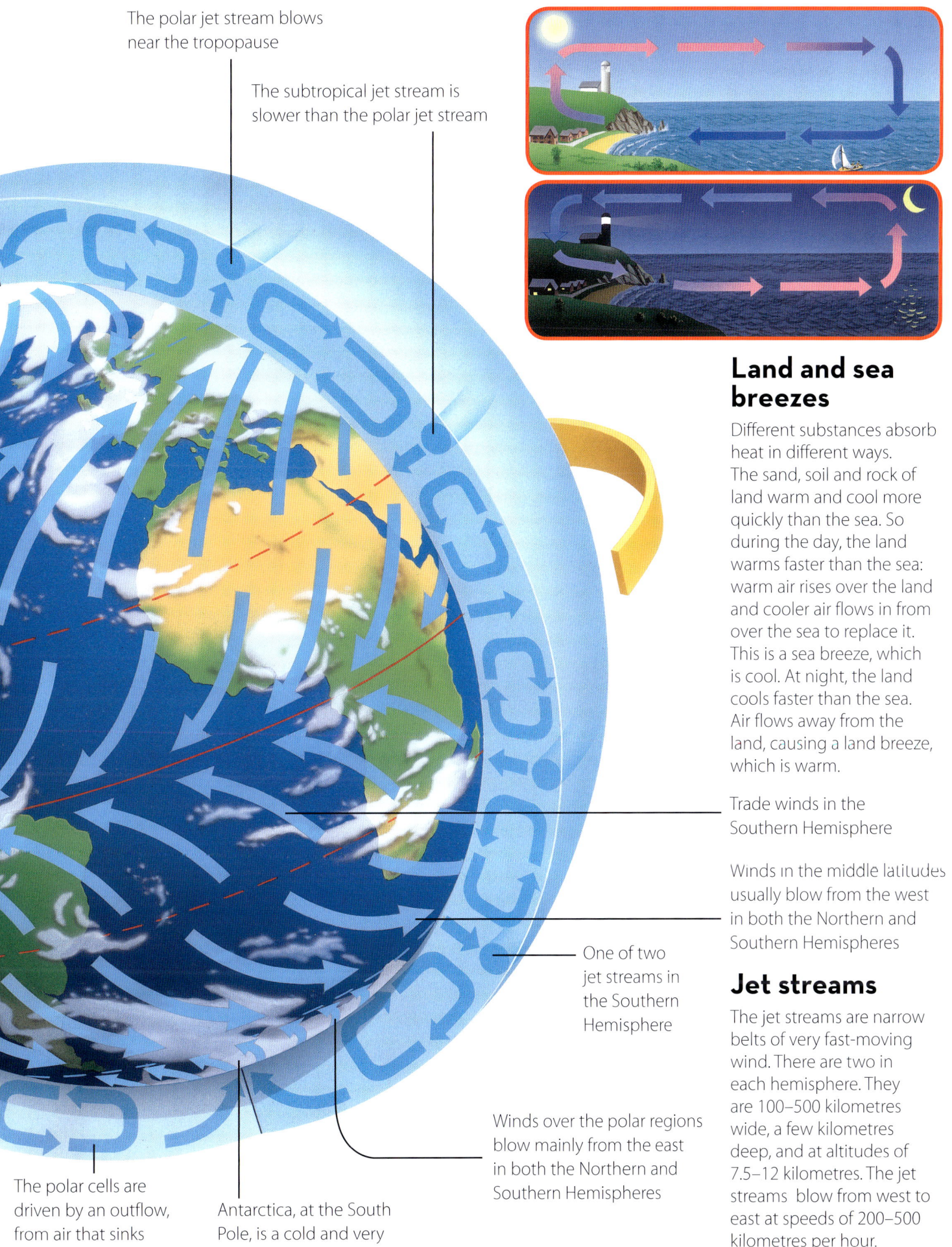

The polar jet stream blows near the tropopause

The subtropical jet stream is slower than the polar jet stream

Trade winds in the Southern Hemisphere

Winds in the middle latitudes usually blow from the west in both the Northern and Southern Hemispheres

One of two jet streams in the Southern Hemisphere

Winds over the polar regions blow mainly from the east in both the Northern and Southern Hemispheres

The polar cells are driven by an outflow, from air that sinks over the poles

Antarctica, at the South Pole, is a cold and very dry desert

Land and sea breezes

Different substances absorb heat in different ways. The sand, soil and rock of land warm and cool more quickly than the sea. So during the day, the land warms faster than the sea: warm air rises over the land and cooler air flows in from over the sea to replace it. This is a sea breeze, which is cool. At night, the land cools faster than the sea. Air flows away from the land, causing a land breeze, which is warm.

Jet streams

The jet streams are narrow belts of very fast-moving wind. There are two in each hemisphere. They are 100–500 kilometres wide, a few kilometres deep, and at altitudes of 7.5–12 kilometres. The jet streams blow from west to east at speeds of 200–500 kilometres per hour.

11

Water World

Water covers more than 70 per cent of the Earth's surface. Most of it is sea water. Only 3 per cent is fresh water, and three quarters of that is in polar regions and permanently frozen. Fresh water reaches the land as fog, dew, hail, rain and snow and is the only water that land-dwelling plants and animals can use. It is called fresh because it has a lower concentration of dissolved salts than sea water. Fresh water is created as sea water evaporates (becomes a gas) and its salt is left behind in the sea.

When water in the sea, lakes, rivers and ground is heated by the Sun and evaporates, it becomes airborne water vapour. It then cools and condenses (turns into water droplets) to form dew, fog and clouds. At ground level, some evaporates again, while the rest drains into rivers and is carried back to the sea. Water is always circulating, from sea to land and back again. This is called the water cycle, or hydrological cycle.

Rainbows

A rainbow appears when light is bent and reflected inside raindrops. The different colours of light are bent by different amounts, so they appear separately.

Water that evaporates from the sea is carried over the land by winds

When air rises and cools, the airborne water vapour condenses to form clouds

Warmed by the Sun, water from the sea evaporates and rises into the air

Water vapour

Water vapour is a gas. Even the driest air contains some water vapour. You cannot see it, smell it, or taste it. It consists of water molecules moving in all directions. Water vapour molecules are separate – each has two hydrogen atoms and one oxygen atom.

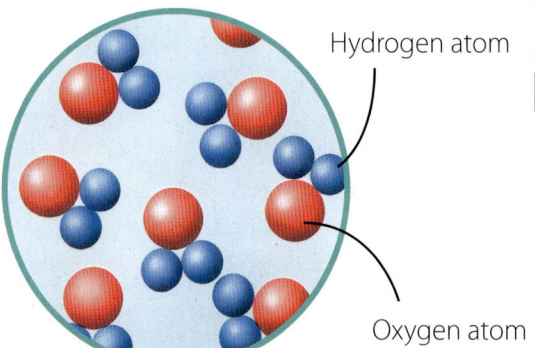

Hydrogen atom

Oxygen atom

A lot of water that falls onto the land drains into rivers which carry the water back to the sea

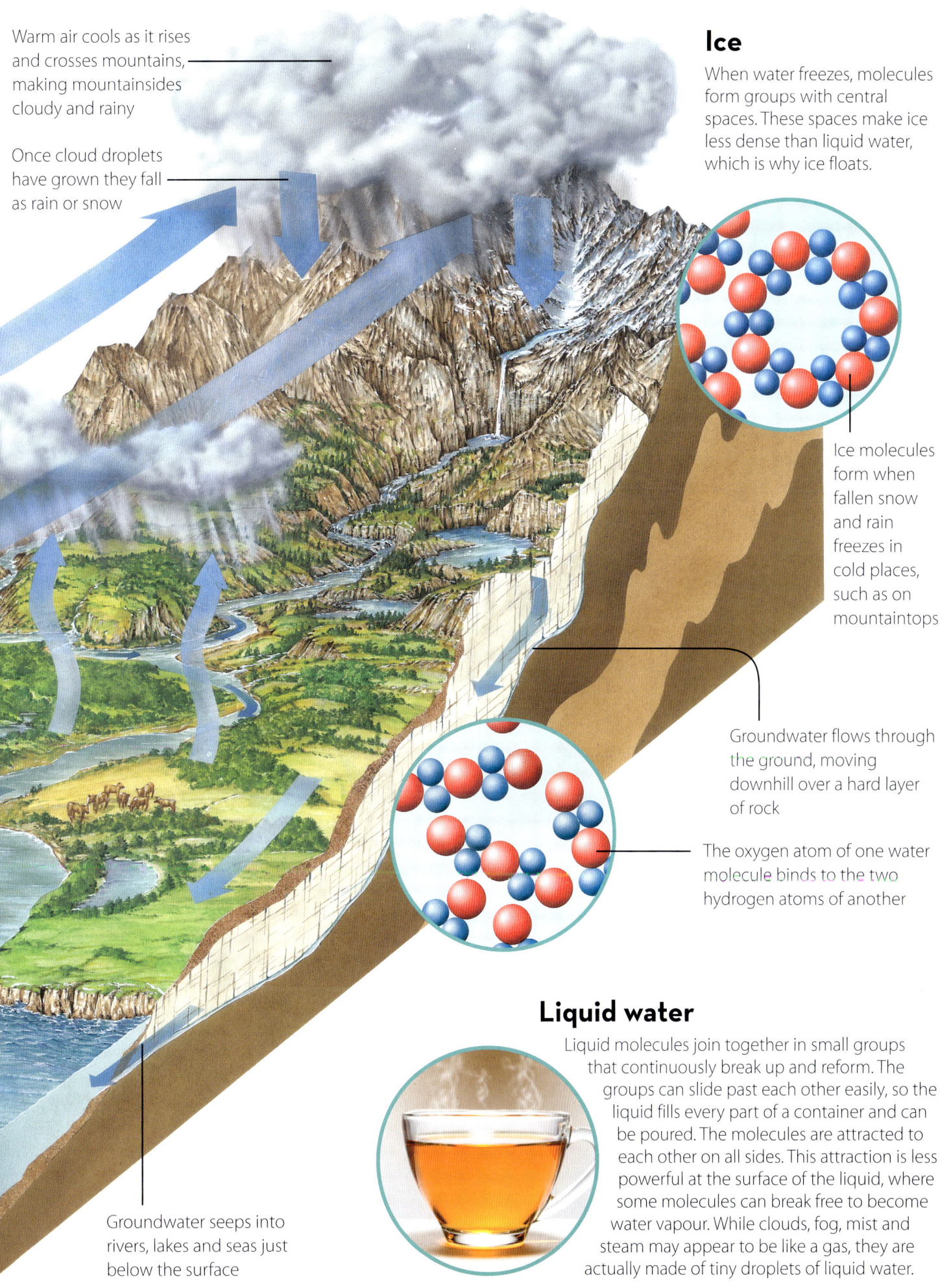

Warm air cools as it rises and crosses mountains, making mountainsides cloudy and rainy

Once cloud droplets have grown they fall as rain or snow

Ice
When water freezes, molecules form groups with central spaces. These spaces make ice less dense than liquid water, which is why ice floats.

Ice molecules form when fallen snow and rain freezes in cold places, such as on mountaintops

Groundwater flows through the ground, moving downhill over a hard layer of rock

The oxygen atom of one water molecule binds to the two hydrogen atoms of another

Groundwater seeps into rivers, lakes and seas just below the surface

Liquid water
Liquid molecules join together in small groups that continuously break up and reform. The groups can slide past each other easily, so the liquid fills every part of a container and can be poured. The molecules are attracted to each other on all sides. This attraction is less powerful at the surface of the liquid, where some molecules can break free to become water vapour. While clouds, fog, mist and steam may appear to be like a gas, they are actually made of tiny droplets of liquid water.

Clouds

Warm air can hold more water than cold air. When warm air cools down, it can't hold as much water, and some of its moisture content may condense into liquid droplets. You can see this happen when the moisture in your warm breath condenses in cold air.

Air temperature decreases with altitude, so as air rises it also becomes cooler. If the rising air is moist, some of the moisture it holds may condense into tiny water droplets that hang in the air. Clouds are made up of many of these droplets. Each droplet is so small that it would take around one million of them to make a single raindrop. Clouds vary – some are flat and smooth, others are fluffy, some are huge and dark. These differences are due to the speed at which the air rises. Smooth sheets of cloud form in air that rises slowly. Storm clouds grow in air that is rising very quickly.

High-level clouds

These clouds form more than 6,000 metres above the Earth's surface, where the air is very cold. The clouds are white and thin, wispy or feathery. They are made up of tiny ice crystals.

Cirrus cloud forms wispy strands

Mid-level clouds

Clouds that form at heights of 2,000 to 6,000 metres have names beginning with 'alto', meaning 'high'. They are made up of water droplets. Light rain or snow can fall from them.

Altocumulus cloud forms small, round patches or rolls of cloud that sometimes merge

Altostratus is smooth, grey cloud that just allows the Sun to show as a glow

Rising air

Air can rise for different reasons. For example, convection (*above, left*). Here, warm land and sea heat the air close to them. This makes the air expand, which causes it to become less dense. Cooler, denser air sinks and pushes the warm air up. Then the cool air is warmed and the process repeats. Orographic lifting ('orographic' means to do with mountains) happens when surface air meets a mountain range and is forced to rise (*centre*). When warm and cold air meet at a front (*right*), they do not mix. Instead, the warm air rises over the cold air.

Stratocumulus are patches or rolls of low-level cloud consisting of water droplets

Vapour trails

Long streams of cloud sometimes stretch out behind an aircraft. The hot exhaust from the engines contains water vapour. The exhaust cools rapidly in the cold air and the water vapour changes directly into crystals of ice.

Cumulonimbus

These are dark, thick clouds that bring heavy showers of rain, snow or hail. Big cumulonimbus clouds (**1**) cause thunderstorms and they can produce tornadoes. The cloud base is near the ground but the top of the cloud can extend up to an altitude of more than 12 kilometres.

Lower-level clouds

Dull, grey clouds that form below 2,000 metres often cover the sky. Their names include 'strat', meaning layer. Stratus is flat, grey, low cloud. Nimbostratus (**2**) is the cloud that is the main cause of light drizzle, rain and snow. Banner cloud stretches downwind from a mountain peak (**3**). Cooling towers can create low-level clouds (**4**). Water used for cooling vaporises and then condenses as it rises above the towers.

Cumulus cloud is separate patches of white, fluffy cloud that often form in fine weather

Highs and Lows

Air expands when it is warmed. Its molecules move further apart and so the air becomes less dense. A column of warm air reaching up from the ground contains fewer molecules than a similar column of cold air, so the warm air weighs less and exerts less pressure. It forms an area of low pressure. If the air is cooled, the opposite happens. Its molecules move closer together, its density increases, and it forms an area of high pressure.

Air moves towards areas of low pressure and away from areas of high pressure. The Earth's rotation then makes the air circulate around the areas of high and low pressure. Warm air and cool air do not mix easily. A boundary, called a front, forms between them. Areas of high and low pressure, and the fronts separating them, produce our weather.

Weather chart

The lines on a weather chart are called isobars. They join places where the pressure is the same. Their patterns reveal centres of high (H) and low (L) pressure. Winds blow roughly parallel to the isobars. Fronts are shown by lines across the isobars. Semicircles indicate a warm front, with warm air behind it. Triangles mark a cold front. Where they meet, cold air is moving beneath warm air and lifting it from the ground. This produces a centre of low pressure called a depression.

Jet stream

Air from the jet stream sinks to produce high pressure near the ground

When there is high pressure near the ground, there is low pressure in the upper air

A cold front

High pressure

High pressure often produces fine weather. Cold air sinks and flows outwards. Surface air flows clockwise around a centre of high pressure in the Northern Hemisphere and anti-clockwise in the Southern. An area of high pressure is called an anticyclone.

An area of high pressure

The higher the pressure is at the centre, the stronger the winds are

Where the flow of air (jet stream) curves towards the Equator, it is called a trough

Rising air flowing into the jet stream produces low pressure (a depression) at ground level

When there is low pressure at ground level, there is high pressure in the upper air

Low pressure

Low pressure often brings cloud and drizzle, rain, or snow. Air moves inwards and rises to merge into the jet stream. As it rises, the air cools and its moisture condenses to form clouds. At the same time, cooler air moves in beneath it, eventually raising it clear of the ground. This produces a depression, also called a cyclone.

When the path of the air curves towards the pole, it is called a ridge

Jet stream

A warm front

Ridge Trough

An area of low pressure

Air flows anticlockwise around low pressure in the Northern Hemisphere and clockwise in the Southern

Cold air pushes beneath the warm air

Ridges and troughs

The jet streams (winds that flow all around the Earth) drag weather systems from west to east. The winds follow wavy paths running in both hemispheres. The curves are caused by the Earth's rotation. When they curve towards the pole, they are ridges; when they curve towards the Equator, they are troughs. Sometimes the ridges become so big that the usual pattern breaks down and the jet streams move in circles. When this happens, the weather does not change for two weeks or more.

Fronts

Cold air is denser than warm air. When the two meet, instead of mixing together, the cold, dense air pushes under the warm air or the warm air rides over the cold air. Eventually, all of the warm air is raised clear of the ground.

The boundary where warm and cold air meet is called a front. If the air behind a moving front is cooler than the air ahead, it is a cold front. If the air behind the front is warmer, it is a warm front. 'Warm' and 'cold' mean only that one mass of air is warm or cool compared with the other. When the warm air begins to be lifted clear of the surface, the cold and warm fronts are said to be occluded. Once they have occluded, both of the fronts slowly disappear.

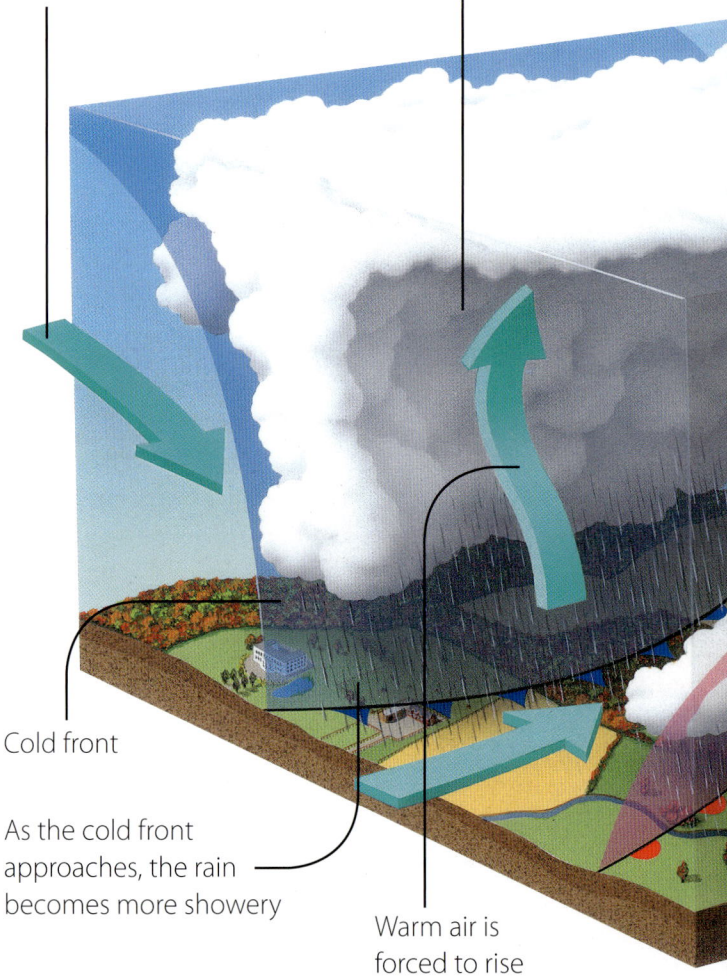

Cold air pushes beneath warm air, producing heaped clouds and showers

There is an area of low pressure where the fronts meet

Cold front

As the cold front approaches, the rain becomes more showery

Warm air is forced to rise

Warm front

Warm fronts are less steep than cold fronts because warm air is less dense than cold air. Warm air moves quite slowly up the front (*bottom left*). Moisture in the air condenses to form sheets of cloud. The lower clouds often bring light but fairly continuous rain, drizzle or snow. The cloud may extend a long way into the warm air behind the front, which can mean several days of dull, wet weather. Because of the slope, cloud also extends a long way ahead of the front. When the first wisps of thin cloud appear high overhead, the place where the front touches the ground may still be up to 400 kilometres away.

Cold front

A cold front is at the leading edge of a mass of cold air (*below, right*). It pushes under the warmer air like a wedge. As the warmer air rises, heaped clouds form, often bringing rain or snow. Because of the slope, clouds along the front are in the warmer air that lies above the colder air. Small, puffy clouds appear lower down in the sky as the front moves away.

It is sometimes possible to see a weather front (*above*).

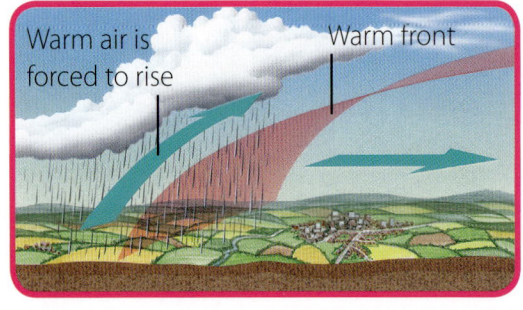

Warm air is forced to rise

Warm front

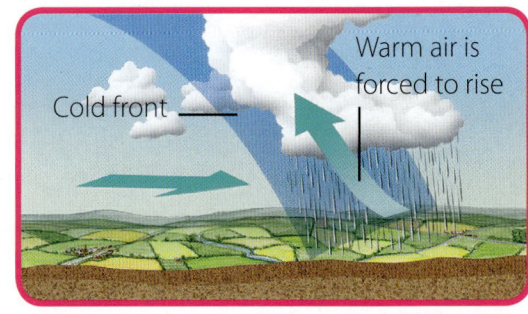

Cold front

Warm air is forced to rise

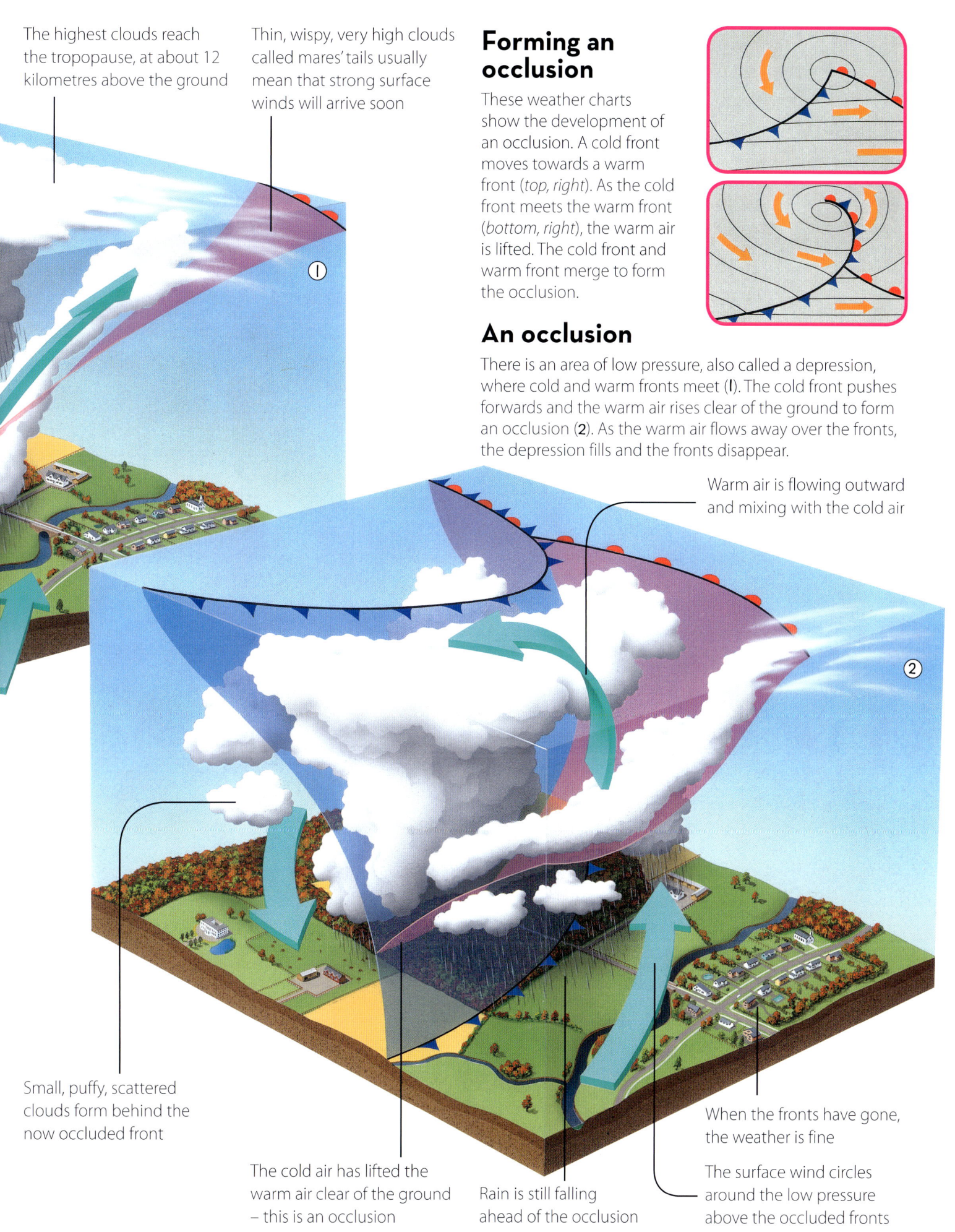

The highest clouds reach the tropopause, at about 12 kilometres above the ground

Thin, wispy, very high clouds called mares' tails usually mean that strong surface winds will arrive soon

Forming an occlusion

These weather charts show the development of an occlusion. A cold front moves towards a warm front (*top, right*). As the cold front meets the warm front (*bottom, right*), the warm air is lifted. The cold front and warm front merge to form the occlusion.

An occlusion

There is an area of low pressure, also called a depression, where cold and warm fronts meet (**1**). The cold front pushes forwards and the warm air rises clear of the ground to form an occlusion (**2**). As the warm air flows away over the fronts, the depression fills and the fronts disappear.

Warm air is flowing outward and mixing with the cold air

Small, puffy, scattered clouds form behind the now occluded front

The cold air has lifted the warm air clear of the ground – this is an occlusion

Rain is still falling ahead of the occlusion

When the fronts have gone, the weather is fine

The surface wind circles around the low pressure above the occluded fronts

Rain and Snow

As warm air cools, some of the moisture it holds condenses into liquid droplets. These form clouds. The droplets are so tiny that they fall very slowly. When they reach drier air, they evaporate, but more moisture condenses to replace them. In large clouds, the droplets can grow. They may merge together or freeze into ice crystals that stick together, making snowflakes. As they grow bigger and heavier, they fall faster. Eventually, they fall out of the cloud. If they reach the ground they are called drizzle, rain, or snow.

Outside of the tropics, most rain consists of snowflakes that have melted in warm air. We only see snow if the air between the cloud and ground is below freezing.

Hailstones

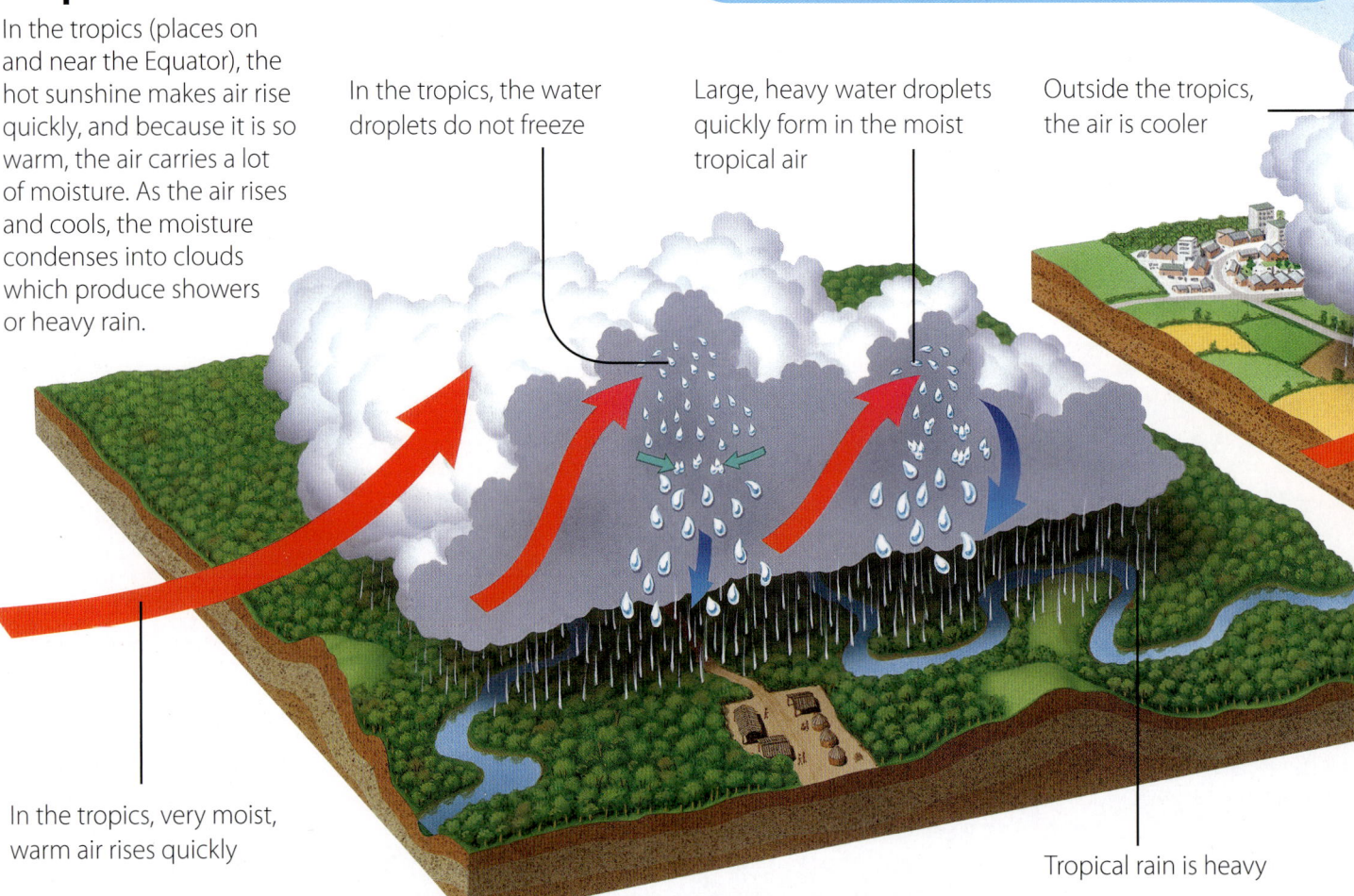

A cross-section of a hailstone

In some storm clouds, pieces of ice are lifted to the top by the air current, then as they fall more moisture condenses on them. They then rise high enough to freeze again. This is how hailstones form and grow, layer by layer (*see above*).

Tropical rain

In the tropics (places on and near the Equator), the hot sunshine makes air rise quickly, and because it is so warm, the air carries a lot of moisture. As the air rises and cools, the moisture condenses into clouds which produce showers or heavy rain.

In the tropics, the water droplets do not freeze

Large, heavy water droplets quickly form in the moist tropical air

Outside the tropics, the air is cooler

In the tropics, very moist, warm air rises quickly

Tropical rain is heavy

Rain and snow clouds

As warm air rises and cools, moisture in the air condenses. This process of condensation releases heat, warming the air and making it rise further, so more moisture condenses. This produces white, fluffy, heaped clouds called cumulus that grow until their tops reach air that is too dry for moisture to condense. Inside each cloud, warm air is rising and cool air is sinking. If a cloud grows big enough, it produces showers of rain (*below, left*) or snow (*below, right*).

At the top of the cloud, water freezes into tiny ice crystals – these form snowflakes

Snowflakes

When an ice crystal falls through moist air, more crystals grow on it. These form the complex patterns of snowflakes. Although no two snowflakes are identical, they always have six sides.

Above this level, the temperature is below freezing

Cool air sinks

Snowflakes continue to grow as they fall

Snowflakes grow best at just below 0 °C

Snow settles when the temperature of the ground is below freezing

Most rain is snow that has melted in the warm air near the base of the cloud

Rising air currents draw more air into the base of the cloud

Snow falls when the air temperature is below 4 °C

Freezing rain

Sometimes the temperature of raindrops is very close to freezing. If they fall onto very cold surfaces they will freeze instantly. This is called freezing rain. It forms a thick layer of clear ice on the ground.

Thunderstorms

If moist air rises fast enough, the moisture content within it can condense into a huge, dark grey storm cloud called cumulonimbus. Inside the cloud, air rises at up to 160 km/h (kilometres per hour). Water freezes near the top of the cloud and small pieces of ice fall back down. The falling ice particles drag cold air behind them, so as well as the warm up-currents, there are also cold down-currents.

The rising and falling ice particles become electrically charged. Quite soon, the upper part of the cloud has a positive charge and the lower part has a negative charge. The negative charge then induces a positive charge on the ground, beneath the cloud. When the difference in the charges is big enough, sparks fly between positive and negative. The sparks are what we see as lightning and hear as thunder.

Wind sweeps the top of the cloud into an anvil shape

The upper part of the cloud has a positive charge

Up-currents carry air and moisture all the way to the tropopause

At this height there are only ice crystals

The huge cloud is made up of ice crystals and water droplets

Thunder

Lightning heats the air so strongly and so quickly that it explodes. Thunder is the sound of the exploding air. It rumbles because the noise takes longer to reach us from the top of the lightning stroke than it does from the bottom.

Lightning typically strikes tall objects on the ground, which can cause fires and split trees

All kinds of lightning

Lightning sparks occur between areas of positive and negative electrical charge. Lightning can flash between a cloud and the ground, or from one cloud to another, or between two parts of the same cloud. If it flashes to the ground (*above, left*), we see it as forked lightning. It may also appear as forked lightning if it flashes between clouds (*above, centre*), although flashes between clouds can also appear as sheet lightning. Lightning inside a cloud appears as a white flash of sheet lightning (*above, right*).

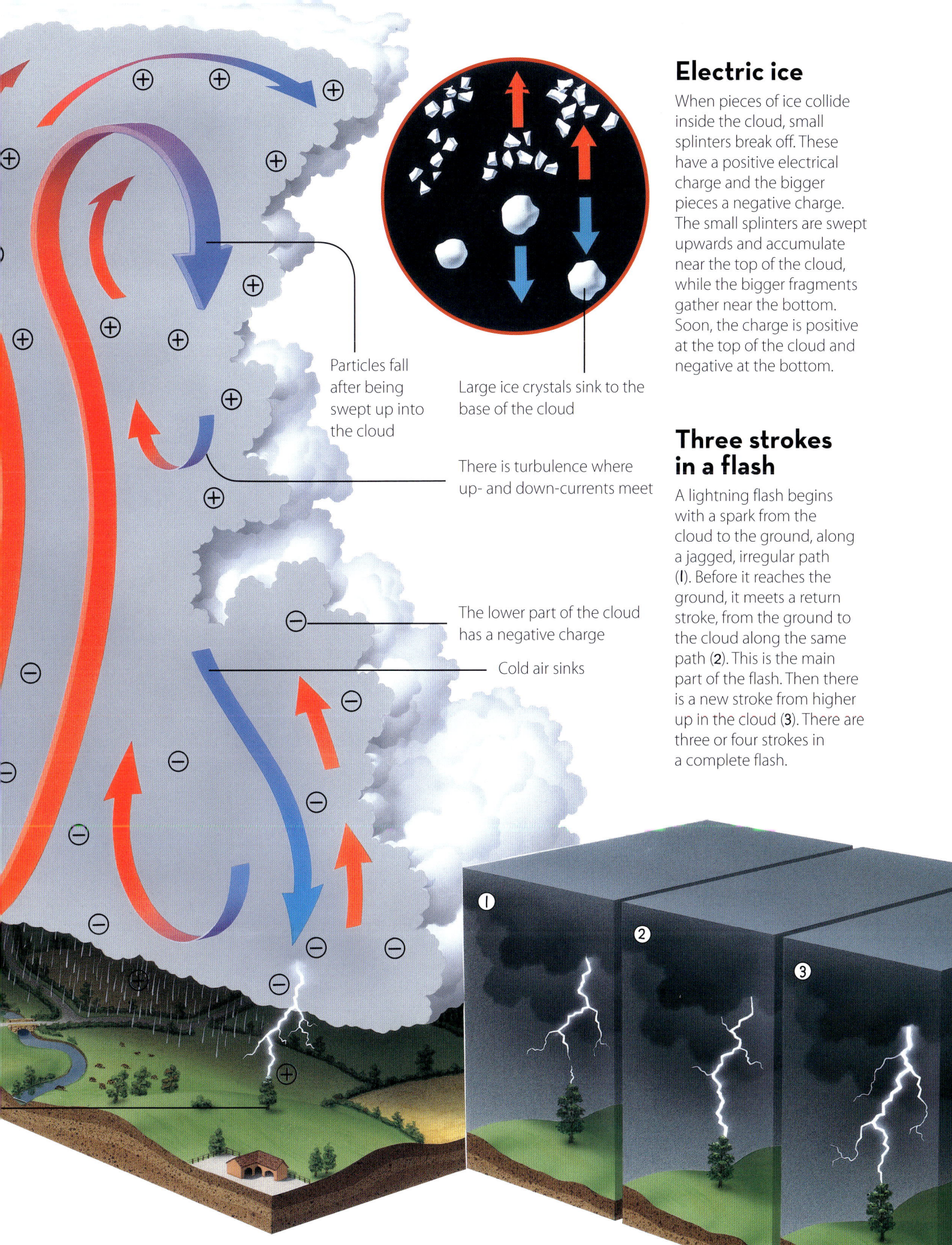

Hurricanes

Hurricanes are the biggest and most violent storms on Earth. They can be 900 kilometres across. The wind speed near the centre of a hurricane is always more than 120 km/h (kilometres per hour), but can be more than 240 km/h. Hurricanes form over the tropical oceans, between about 190 and 775 kilometres north or south of the Equator. The sea temperature must be at least 27 °C and there must be a disturbance in the flow of air to set it turning.

A hurricane begins to form as warm, moist air rises rapidly. Huge storm clouds grow as moisture in the air condenses. Once the mass of warm air starts to turn, air that is drawn into the base of the clouds spirals upwards. A hurricane usually begins on the eastern side of an ocean and travels westward. Then it curves along a track that takes it away from the Equator.

Inside a hurricane

Spiralling air produces a central ring of cloud with a cloud-free centre, called the eye. Beyond this lies a circle fairly clear of cloud (where the air is sinking), then a more cloudy circle (where the air is rising). The pattern is repeated outwards, but with the clouds becoming more scattered further away from the centre.

The wind changes direction above the storm

As well as the wind, a hurricane brings prolonged and torrential rain

There are huge waves

Storm surge

The low pressure at the centre of a hurricane causes the sea level to rise and the fierce winds produce big waves. When the storm reaches a coast, these combine to carry water inland, sometimes for several kilometres. The biggest hurricanes can raise the sea to more than 15 metres above its normal level. This is called a storm surge.

The wind carries away the rising air, drawing more air from below

Seen from space
Satellites in orbit are used to photograph and monitor hurricanes, such as Hurricane Florence (*right*). This allows scientists to follow their movements and wind strength.

The warm air cools as it rises, then sinks

Near the hurricane's edge, clouds are scattered

Between the bands of cloud, air is sinking

Rings of cloud develop where the warm, moist air is rising

The sea is calm beneath the eye

The entire hurricane is turning, making the wind stronger and the sea stormier on one side

Eye of the storm
Inside the eye there is little cloud, almost no wind, and the air is warm. The descending air produces the clear skies., but there is great danger just outside it. The eye is surrounded by stormy seas and high winds.

Tornadoes

Tornadoes are the fiercest and most destructive of all winds. Descending from a storm cloud, a column of rotating air becomes a tornado when it touches the ground. Air is drawn into the tornado funnel and spirals upwards. This generates a wind around the centre of at least 65 km/h (kilometres per hour) and occasionally more than 500 km/h. Tornadoes are rarely wider than about 350 metres at the base and many are smaller. The wider the funnel, the stronger the winds inside.

Most tornadoes follow an erratic path over the ground, travelling at 40–65 km/h but sometimes at up to 100 km/h. Some remain stationary. Few tornadoes last longer than about twenty minutes and many disappear after one minute or less, but occasionally one survives for several hours.

Inside the cloud, falling hail, snow and rain drag cold air down

Torrential rain falls

Air is rising at 100 km/h or more

The tornado leaves a narrow trail of destruction

Outside the path of the tornado, rain and huge hailstones often cause serious damage, especially to farm crops

Life of a tornado

A tornado is born when the centre of a huge storm cloud starts to rotate. This section then extends downwards and sticks out beneath the cloud as a wall cloud (**1**). Part of the wall cloud then grows downwards, forming a funnel of twisting air that becomes a tornado when it touches the ground (**2**). Dust and debris drawn into the funnel darken it (**3**) and the tornado throws out debris at high speed. Once a tornado lifts from the ground, it is harmless (**4**), but it can touch down again.

Bulges at the bottom of the storm cloud are called mammatus

The funnel of air spirals upwards

The funnel snakes across the ground

Waterspouts

If a tornado crosses water, it becomes a waterspout. Waterspouts can also form over water. As air is drawn into a waterspout, the low pressure makes its moisture condense into droplets. It is the droplets that make the funnel visible, so waterspouts are always white. They are less violent than tornadoes that form over land but can damage small boats.

Tiny but fierce tornadoes, called suction vortices, sometimes form around the main tornado

Destruction

Tornadoes throw cars around like toys and can demolish houses. A violent tornado can overturn a railway train and strip the bark from trees before uprooting them. It will reduce whole areas to scattered rubble.

Objects can be lifted right into the cloud and then dropped again

Wind and Water

Air moving away from the Equator carries warmth into the far north and south, spreading the heat more evenly. This movement produces winds near the Earth's surface. Over the oceans, the winds push the sea water. Moving water, driven by the wind, forms ocean currents.

Warm equatorial currents flow from east to west on either side of the Equator in the Pacific, Atlantic and Indian oceans. These surface currents are driven by the trade winds, which blow from the northeast in the Northern Hemisphere and the southeast in the Southern Hemisphere. In the Pacific Ocean the winds sometimes change and become weaker or stronger, or even reverse and blow in the opposite direction. This can seriously affect the weather along the Pacific coastlines.

La Niña

Sometimes the Pacific trade winds strengthen and the warm Equatorial Current moves faster. This is called La Niña (Spanish for 'little girl'). It causes very dry weather in South America and heavy rain in Indonesia.

During La Niña, storm clouds gather off the coast of Indonesia

The trade winds drive warm surface water westwards

The circulating air flows back at high altitude

Reversed trade winds bring dry weather to Indonesia and Australia

The trade winds usually drive the Equatorial Currents in an east to west direction

The Benguela Current cools air crossing it, producing the dry climate of the Namib Desert

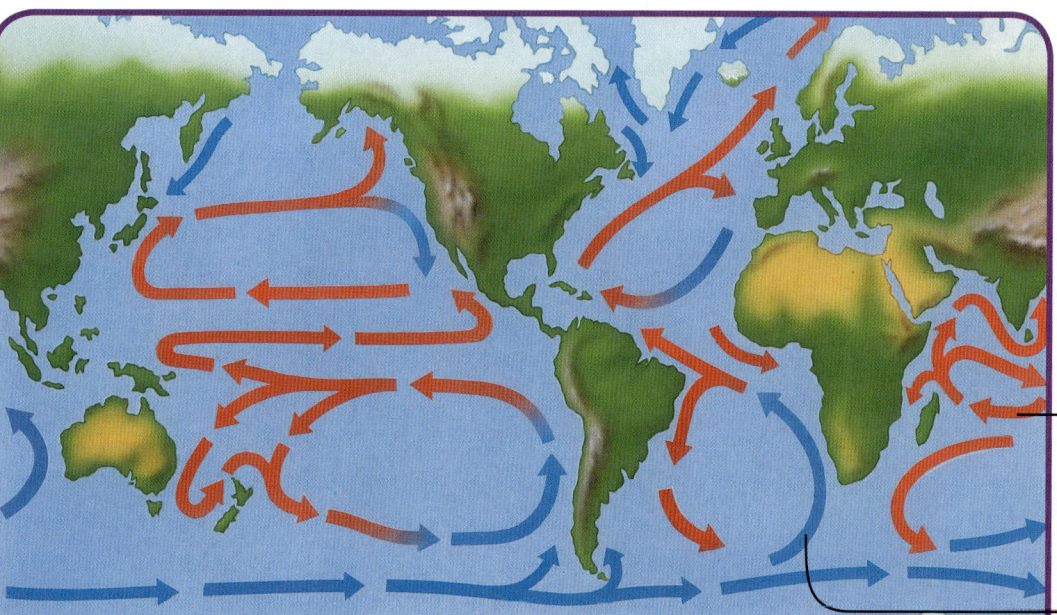

Ocean currents

In each of the oceans, the currents flow roughly in a circle, called a gyre. Warm currents (red arrows, *above*) and cold currents (blue arrows) affect the temperatures and the weather in coastal areas. For example, the cold Benguela Current affects the climate of the Namib Desert in southern Africa.

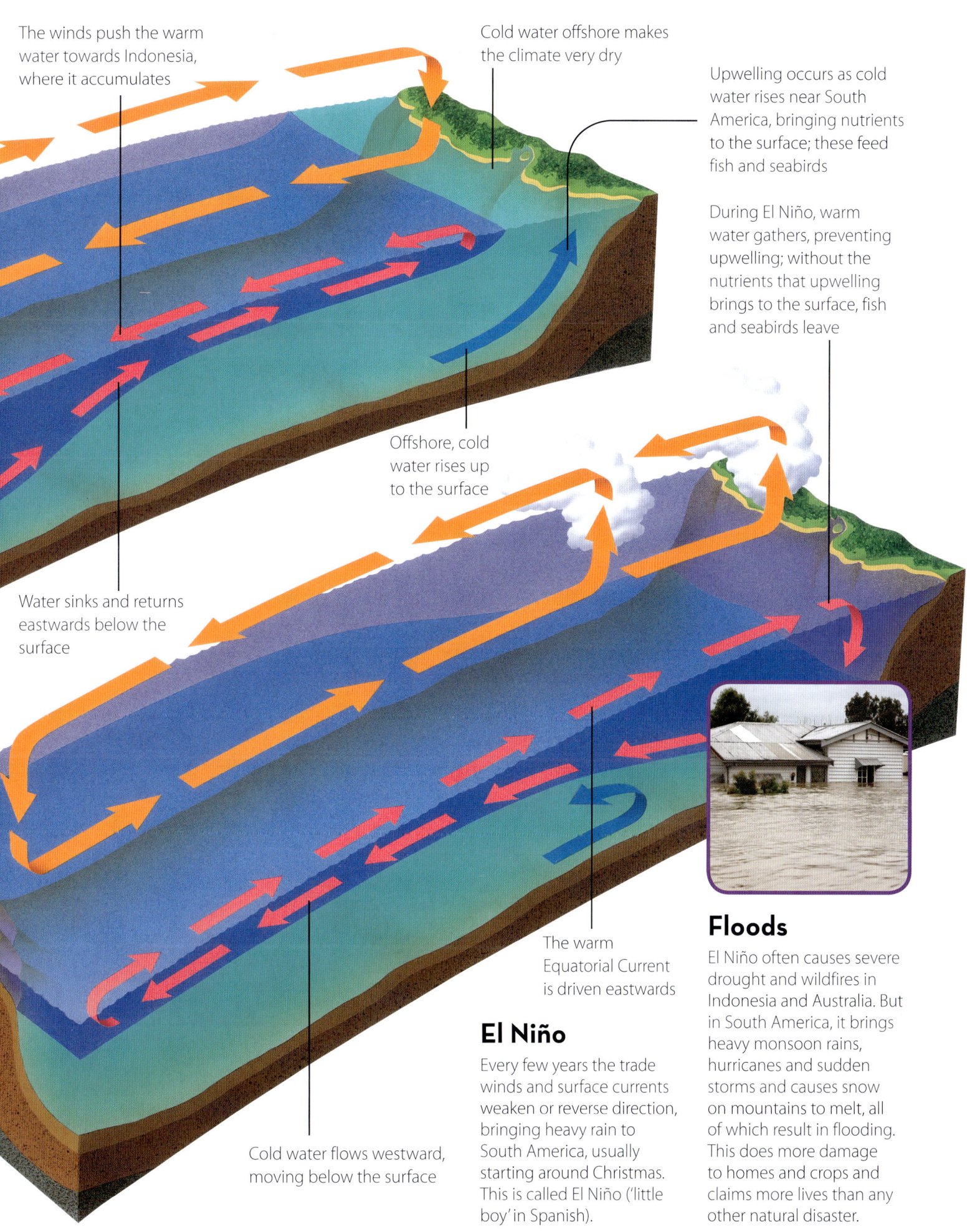

The winds push the warm water towards Indonesia, where it accumulates

Cold water offshore makes the climate very dry

Upwelling occurs as cold water rises near South America, bringing nutrients to the surface; these feed fish and seabirds

During El Niño, warm water gathers, preventing upwelling; without the nutrients that upwelling brings to the surface, fish and seabirds leave

Offshore, cold water rises up to the surface

Water sinks and returns eastwards below the surface

The warm Equatorial Current is driven eastwards

Cold water flows westward, moving below the surface

El Niño

Every few years the trade winds and surface currents weaken or reverse direction, bringing heavy rain to South America, usually starting around Christmas. This is called El Niño ('little boy' in Spanish).

Floods

El Niño often causes severe drought and wildfires in Indonesia and Australia. But in South America, it brings heavy monsoon rains, hurricanes and sudden storms and causes snow on mountains to melt, all of which result in flooding. This does more damage to homes and crops and claims more lives than any other natural disaster.

Measuring

People have always needed to forecast the weather, but until modern times they have had very little to help them. They could watch the skies and see, for example, how the cirrus cloud called mares' tails often meant strong winds were on their way, and how the day after a red sunset was usually fine. They noticed how the direction of the wind was linked to whether the wind brought warm or cold, wet or dry air. They also relied on clues from plants and animals, but these indicators were not very reliable.

Today, we can predict the weather much more accurately because we have instruments to measure temperature, pressure, humidity (how much moisture the air holds), wind speed and direction, rainfall and sunshine brightness. These measurements are taken at ground level from weather stations all over the world, and also at various altitudes throughout the atmosphere using weather balloons.

Beaufort wind scale

The 13-point Beaufort wind scale is used to describe the force of a wind. It relates the force to the wind's visible effects, such as whether branches are being broken off trees. Force 0 means no wind. Force 1 is 'light air' (up to 5 km/h). Force 2–6 winds are breezes (6 to 50 km/h). Winds of force 7–10 are gales (50 to 100 km/h). Force 11 is a storm (100 to 120 km/h). Force 12 is a hurricane (more than 120 km/h).

Fully extended, the cable is 30 metres long

The balloon bursts 20 to 30 kilometres up – this parachute allows the instruments to land safely

A lightweight box contains a radiosonde, which has instruments to measure temperature, pressure and humidity

The radiosonde also contains a radio transmitter to send data back to the weather station

Natural indicators

Some plants respond to weather conditions. Pine cones open in dry weather and close in damp or wet conditions. Seaweed is dry and brittle when the air is dry, but absorbs moisture from the air and becomes soft when the air is more humid. Scarlet pimpernel and morning glory are wild flowers that open when it is sunny and close when the sky is cloudy. However, natural indicators such as these show only the present conditions, not the coming weather. It is not possible to base forecasts on these indicators.

Weather balloons are filled with helium gas and released twice a day from hundreds of points around the world.

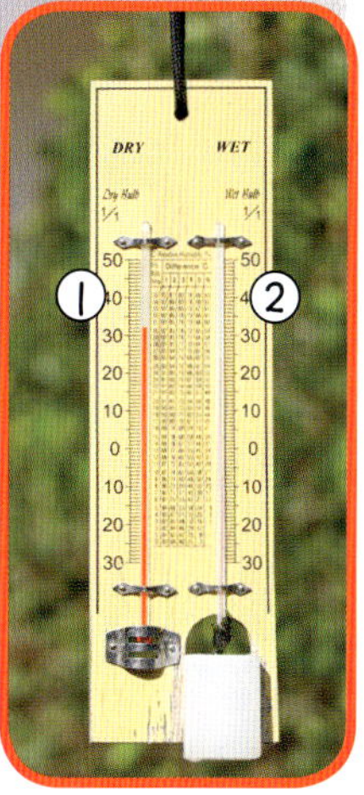

The balloon measures aproximately 1.5 metres across when it is released

The wind spins the cups around their axis

This instrument (called an anemometer) measures wind speed

The speed of the spinning axis is used to calculate the wind speed

The movement of the shaft shows the direction of the wind

The data on wind direction and speed is sent to a computer inside the weather station

The vane aligns itself with the wind direction

More instruments

The difference between the temperatures shown by the dry-bulb (1) and wet-bulb (2) thermometers is used to calculate the relative humidity and dewpoint (the temperature at which moisture in the air condenses). A rain gauge (3) measures the amount of rainfall. A traditional weather vane (4), usually mounted on a tall building, shows the wind direction. A barograph (5) is a barometer linked to a pen and rotating drum that makes a permanent record of changing air pressure. A sunshine recorder (6) focuses sunlight onto a paper. As the Sun crosses the sky, this makes a line of scorch marks, recording the hours of sunshine during the day.

Satellites

The world's first weather satellite, TIROS-1, was launched into orbit by the United States on 1 April 1960. Later models were called NOAA-class satellites. These satellites are in polar orbits. Each one can see a strip of the Earth's surface 3,000 kilometres wide and passes over the entire surface of the Earth in 24 hours.

Today, there are many weather satellites orbiting the Earth, launched by Japan, India, China, Russia, South Korea and Europe as well as the United States. Between them they monitor the whole of the atmosphere all the time, transmitting their measurements and pictures to receiving stations in several countries. Satellites measure temperatures, winds, the area covered by ice and changes in surface vegetation. This information helps scientists to understand and predict the weather and its effects.

Geostationary orbit

A satellite travelling at 11,300 km/h at an altitude of 36,000 kilometres takes exactly 24 hours to complete each orbit. This is the time it takes the Earth to complete one revolution, so the satellite remains above the same position on the surface. It is then in a geostationary orbit. Between them, five weather satellites in equatorial geostationary orbit monitor the entire surface of the Earth.

Meteosat

The first Meteosat Second Generation satellite was built and launched by the European Space Agency into geostationary orbit over the Equator at 0° longitude. The satellite is 3.2 metres long and 2.1 metres wide. It spins at 100 revolutions per minute and lies on its side, with its 'nose' pointing north.

Information from Meteosat satellites is transmitted to a base in Darmstadt, Germany

Solar panels generate electricity from sunlight to supply power for the equipment

The radiometer measures visible and infrared radiation

One of the four VHF radio communications antennae

More radio antennae are housed inside this casing

One of the transmitting antennae around the outside of the communications unit

This unit sends signals to the VHF antennae

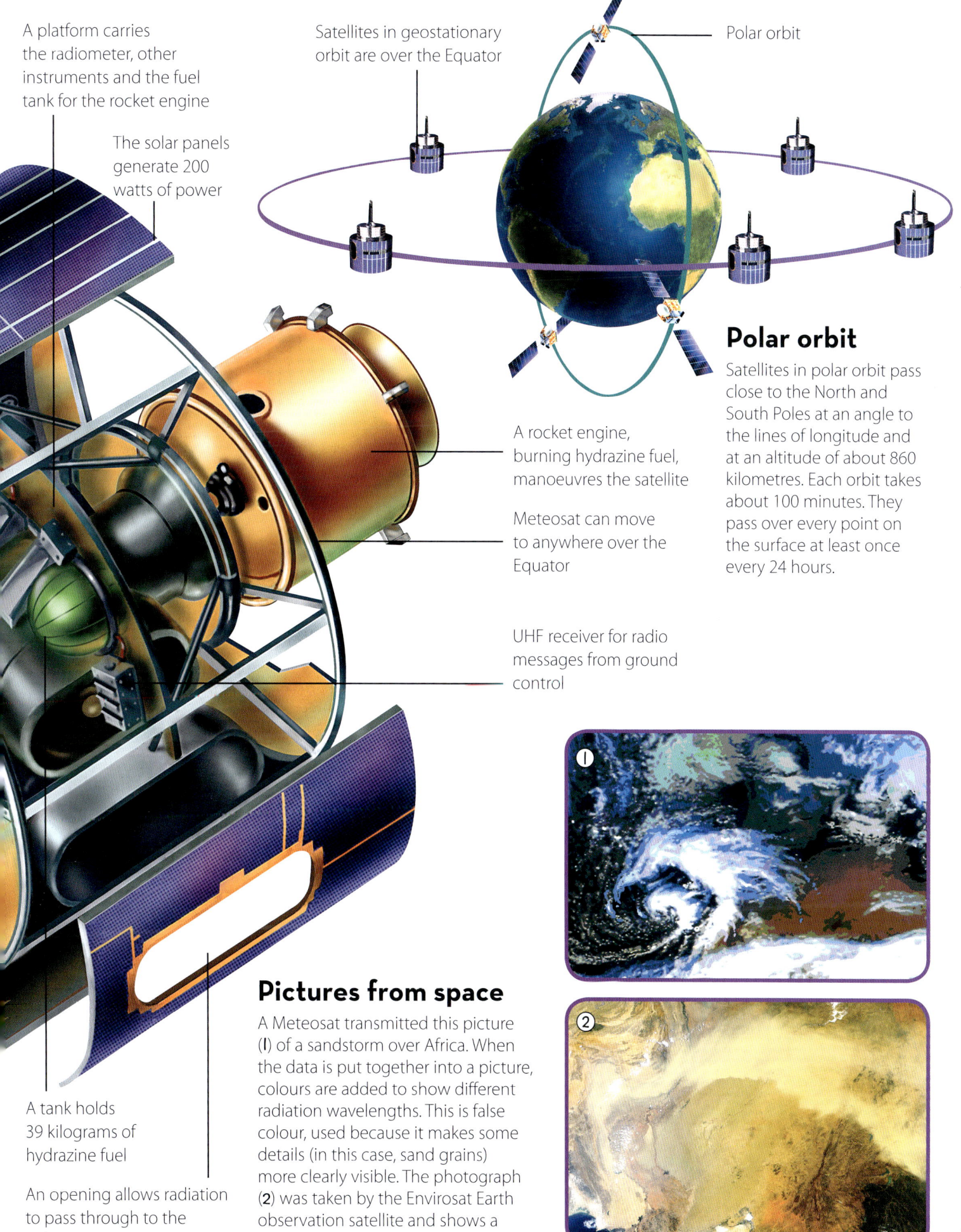

A platform carries the radiometer, other instruments and the fuel tank for the rocket engine

The solar panels generate 200 watts of power

Satellites in geostationary orbit are over the Equator

Polar orbit

A rocket engine, burning hydrazine fuel, manoeuvres the satellite

Meteosat can move to anywhere over the Equator

UHF receiver for radio messages from ground control

A tank holds 39 kilograms of hydrazine fuel

An opening allows radiation to pass through to the radiometer

Polar orbit

Satellites in polar orbit pass close to the North and South Poles at an angle to the lines of longitude and at an altitude of about 860 kilometres. Each orbit takes about 100 minutes. They pass over every point on the surface at least once every 24 hours.

Pictures from space

A Meteosat transmitted this picture (1) of a sandstorm over Africa. When the data is put together into a picture, colours are added to show different radiation wavelengths. This is false colour, used because it makes some details (in this case, sand grains) more clearly visible. The photograph (2) was taken by the Envirosat Earth observation satellite and shows a sandstorm in natural colours.

33

Forecasts

Weather forecasts shown on television last for only a few minutes – long enough for the presenter to tell viewers whether it will be sunny or cloudy, fine or wet, and whether to expect strong winds, flooding, snow or ice. Radio and online weather forecasts typically give more detailed information, and there are also special services for industries that are heavily affected by the weather, such as farming and fishing. Airports may employ professional meteorologists to compile weather forecasts for aviation.

All forecasts are based on data sent from thousands of weather stations on land and at sea, from ships and buoys, and aircraft on routine flights. Specialsed weather aircraft send details of individual weather systems and satellites in orbit high above the Earth transmit a constant stream of measurements.

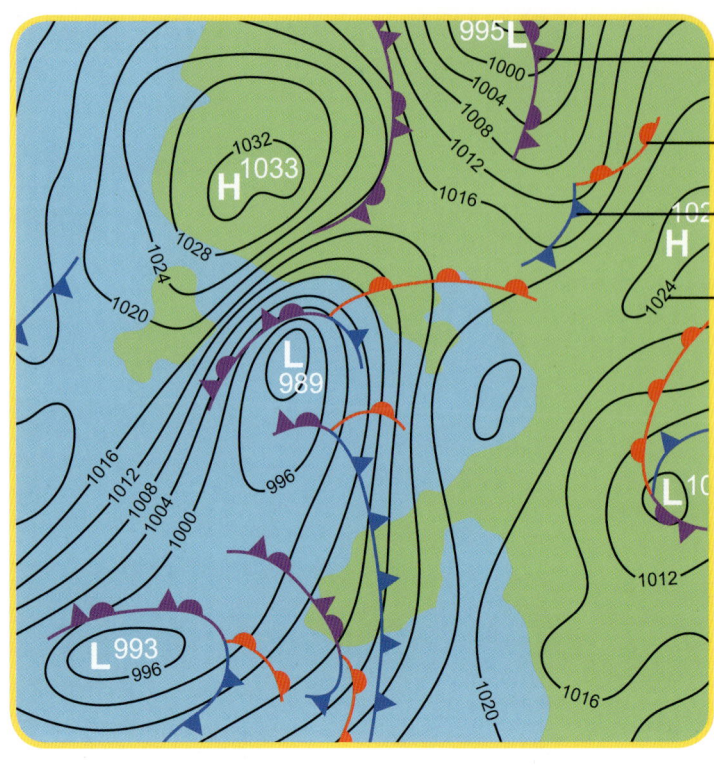

Synoptic chart
Meteorologists prepare synoptic charts to show weather conditions over a large area.

The lines are isobars, joining places where surface air pressure is the same. Centres of high and low pressure are marked. Warm and cold weather fronts cross the isobars. The chart is updated every few hours to show where and how fast the weather is moving.

Satellite pictures of cloud types and patterns show the movement of weather

TV weather forecast
A TV forecast gives an outline of weather conditions over a large area for the next 24 hours. It may also provide a more general forecast for up to three days. It is not possible to accurately forecast what the weather will be more than about a week in advance. The forecast may be presented by a professional meteorologist, but sometimes it is a non-expert reading a script.

Solar cells generate power for the satellite's equipment

Standard symbols show sunshine, cloud, showers, storms or continuous rain

Ships send measurements of air and sea surface temperature and other weather conditions to a forecasting centre

— Occluded front

— Warm front

— Cold front

— The air pressure is shown in millibars

Recording the weather

Weather satellites (1, 2) can measure air and sea temperatures and cloud, snow and ice cover. They can even measure the height of waves on the sea. They transmit the information to surface receiving stations (3) where it is used in preparing forecasts and also for research. Information is sent to weather stations from numerous other sources too. Weather balloons (4) are sent up from hundreds of places around the world every day to collect data from high in the atmosphere. Aircraft fitted with sensitive instruments and radar (5), measure conditions inside weather systems, such as depressions. Many instruments are also used in ground level stations (*see* pages 30–31). The instruments are often housed in a special type of box called a Stevenson screen (6).

Weather buoys at sea report weather conditions automatically

Pollution

An airborne substance that can harm people or other living organisms is called a pollutant. It may be in the form of a gas, liquid particles, or solid particles. Wind and rain can carry pollutants many kilometres from their source. Certain weather conditions, such as intense sunshine and temperature inversion (see right), can make pollution worse in our cities.

Some pollutants occur naturally. For example, volcanoes eject gases and ash. We can do nothing about these, but we can try to reduce the pollution we cause ourselves. Many industrial processes produce substances that can pollute the air if they are not captured before they escape. Car exhausts also cause pollution. We can reduce this by making fewer journeys, using public transport or by driving hybrid cars powered by petrol and electricity or fully electric cars.

Polluted cities

Pollution is usually worst over cities, where there are more sources of pollution. If there is a temperature inversion (when hot air traps cold air below it), the pollutants cannot disperse. This can hold pollution over a city for days. In some places around the world, people wear face masks to protect themselves against the health risks of breathing polluted air.

Sometimes, warm air lies above cooler air and a dome forms where pollutants become trapped

Cool air moves in from the nearby countryside

Acid rain

Burning some kinds of coal and oil releases sulphur dioxide and nitrogen oxides. These gases can be carried a long way by the wind. While they are airborne, they react with oxygen and water, and eventually form tiny droplets of sulphuric and nitric acid that dissolve in cloud droplets or stick to solids. This pollution is called acid rain. It can harm plants and make lakes and rivers acidic.

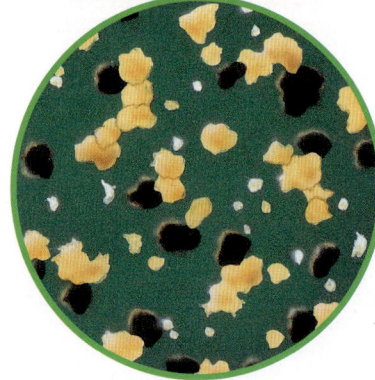

Cement dust

Cement production involves crushing and grinding rock into fine powder. This creates tiny dust particles that can pollute the air. Cement dust release is strictly controlled in most parts of the world as it makes people cough and wheeze, especially if they have asthma, and can cause bronchitis.

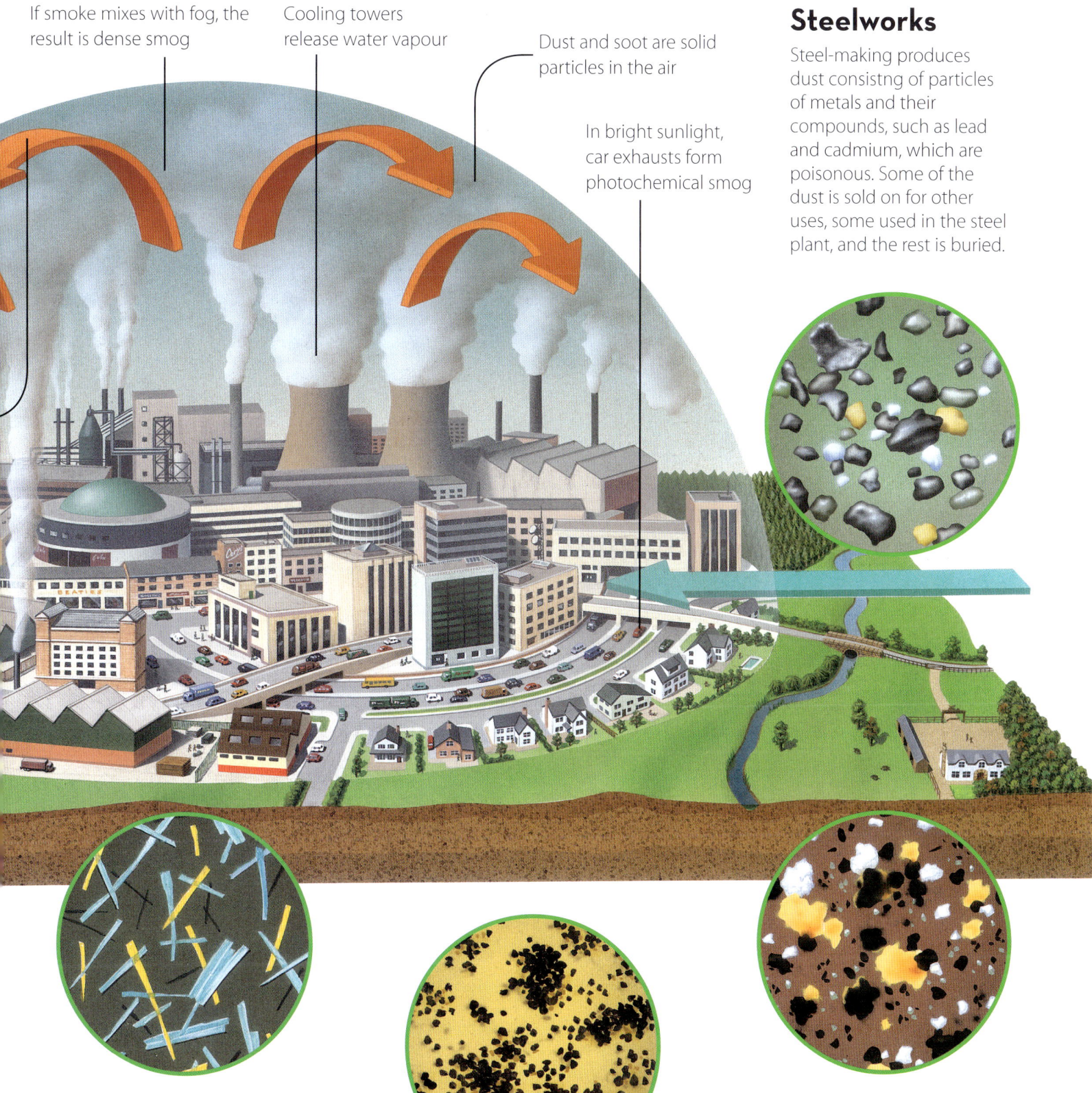

If smoke mixes with fog, the result is dense smog

Cooling towers release water vapour

Dust and soot are solid particles in the air

In bright sunlight, car exhausts form photochemical smog

Steelworks

Steel-making produces dust consistng of particles of metals and their compounds, such as lead and cadmium, which are poisonous. Some of the dust is sold on for other uses, some used in the steel plant, and the rest is buried.

Asbestos

Asbestos is a mineral made from fibrous particles. It was once used for fireproofing and to make roofs and brake linings. Inhaling the fibres can cause serious lung damage. Its use is now banned in most countries.

Car exhaust

As well as exhaust gases, vehicles powered by petrol or diesel engines emit small particles of unburnt fuel. Inhaling these can damage the lungs. In strong sunlight they react with the exhaust gases to form photochemical smog that is also harmful to health.

Powerplants

Coal-burning powerplants produce fly ash as a waste product. It consists of very fine grains of a variety of minerals. It can be harmful if inhaled, but it has a number of industrial uses, so it is collected.

Changing Climate

Sunlight passes straight through the air, all the way to the Earth's surface. It warms the land and sea surface, and when these are warmed, they radiate heat. Certain gases that are naturally present in the atmosphere absorb, and so trap, some of this outgoing heat. This is called the 'greenhouse effect' and without it the world would be very much colder than it is. The gases that absorb the heat include water vapour, carbon dioxide, methane, ozone and nitrous oxide.

Human activity adds to the quantities of some of these greenhouse gases, and Earth's average temperature is increasing. This is global warming, which contributes to changes in our climate. By replacing fossil fuels with renewable sources of energy such as solar and wind power, and by reducing waste, we can help to limit the increase in greenhouse gases.

Sunlight

The Sun radiates light and heat. Its strongest radiation is at the short wavelengths we see as visible light. This radiation passes through the air, but is reflected by clouds.

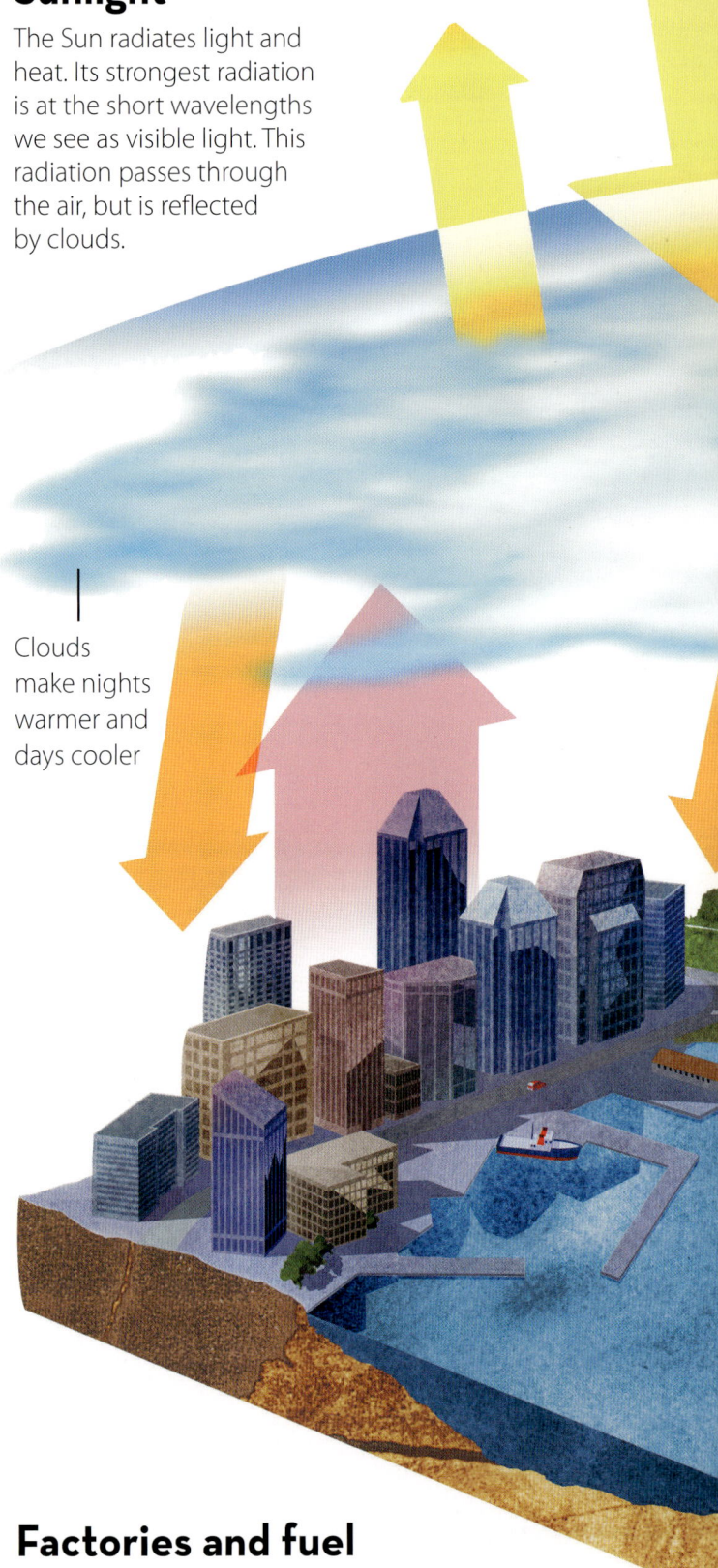

Clouds make nights warmer and days cooler

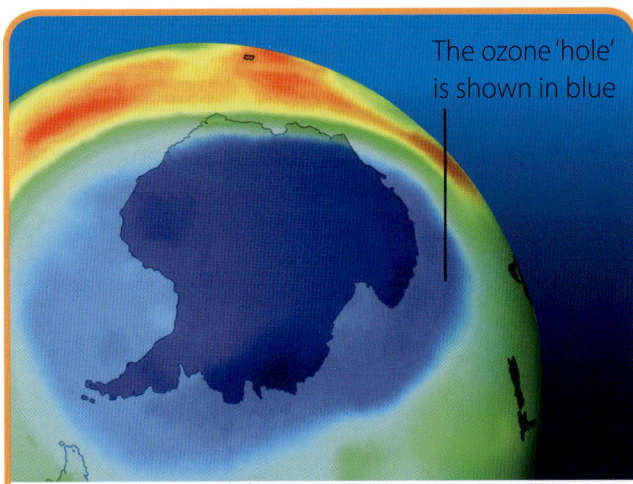

The ozone 'hole' is shown in blue

Ozone 'hole'

Ultraviolet radiation from the Sun can cause skin cancer. The ozone gas layer in the stratosphere protects us by absorbing some of the radiation. Some industrial chemicals reduce the amount of ozone, and this effect is mainly seen over Antarctica in spring. These chemicals are no longer used and it is hoped the ozone layer will eventually recover.

Factories and fuel

Burning coal, oil and gas releases carbon dioxide into the atmosphere. Factories are working to reduce the amount they release by using fuel more efficiently. Reducing waste means using less fuel. Gas releases less carbon dioxide when burned than oil or coal. Conventional power stations release carbon dioxide gas, but nuclear plants emit none at all. Oil companies are developing alternatives to fossil fuels to reduce greenhouse gas emissions.

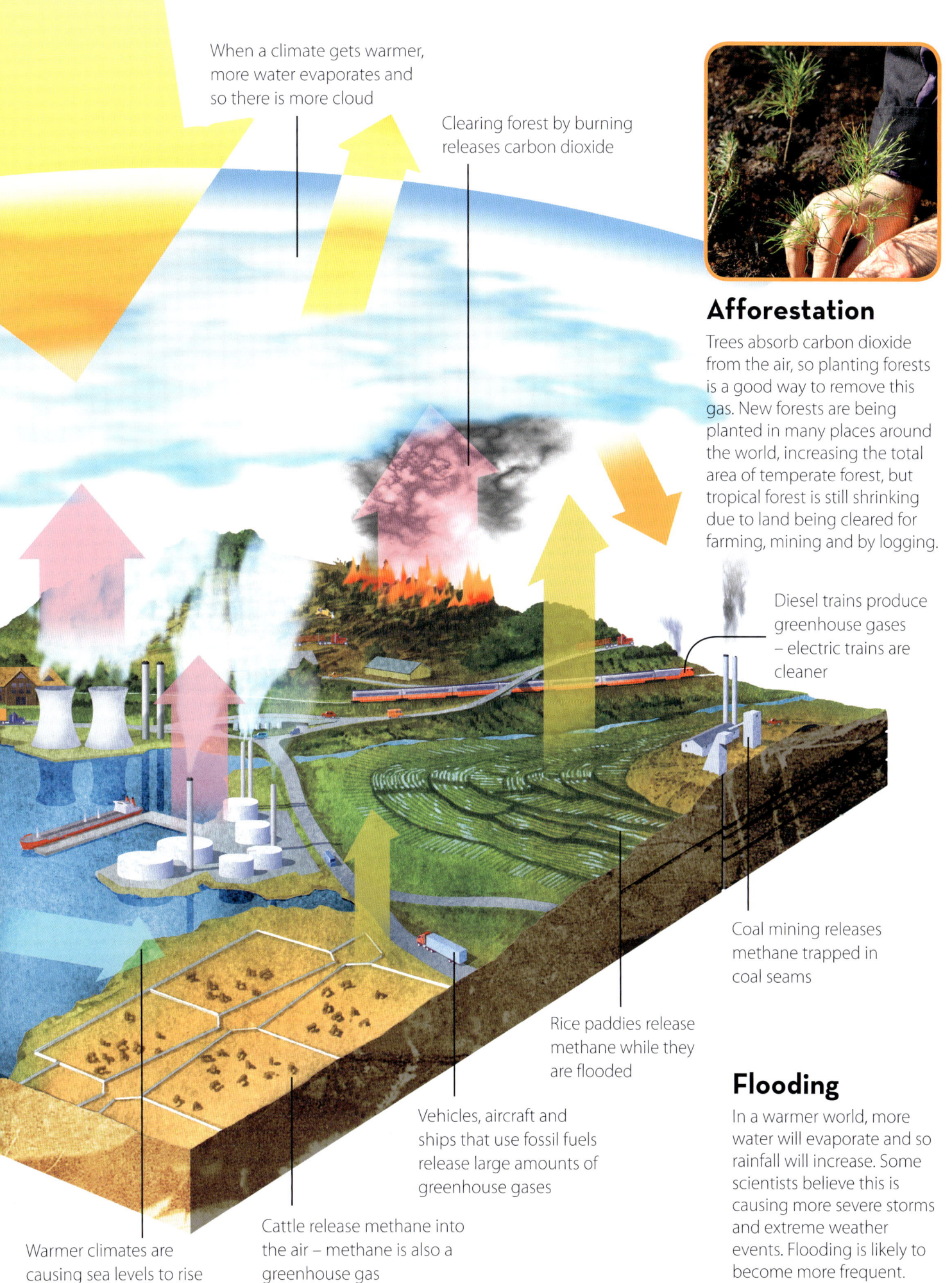

When a climate gets warmer, more water evaporates and so there is more cloud

Clearing forest by burning releases carbon dioxide

Afforestation

Trees absorb carbon dioxide from the air, so planting forests is a good way to remove this gas. New forests are being planted in many places around the world, increasing the total area of temperate forest, but tropical forest is still shrinking due to land being cleared for farming, mining and by logging.

Diesel trains produce greenhouse gases – electric trains are cleaner

Coal mining releases methane trapped in coal seams

Rice paddies release methane while they are flooded

Flooding

In a warmer world, more water will evaporate and so rainfall will increase. Some scientists believe this is causing more severe storms and extreme weather events. Flooding is likely to become more frequent.

Vehicles, aircraft and ships that use fossil fuels release large amounts of greenhouse gases

Cattle release methane into the air – methane is also a greenhouse gas

Warmer climates are causing sea levels to rise

Protection

The houses we live in and the clothes we wear keep us warm and dry. We can look out of the window at the rain pouring down, or the snow piling ever higher in drifts, while staying safe and comfortable. We are protected from the weather.

Rain, snow and wind are features of ordinary weather, but the weather can be extraordinary, and then we need additional protection. Snow avalanches can sweep away houses. Hurricanes can cause storm surges that send water far inland to flood homes and businesses. Rivers can overflow and heavy rain can loosen the earth, causing landslides and mudslides. A lack of rain also brings danger. Extreme heat can kill and prolonged drought can ruin farmers' crops and livelihoods. To tackle these threats, we have found many ways to protect ourselves from the weather.

Flood plains

A river meanders slowly as it crosses fairly level ground. The area covered by the meanders is the river's flood plain. The meanders advance down the plain and the river overflows its banks after heavy rain or when snow melts in spring. As a result, the plain may flood from time to time.

Dams

Opening and closing a dam regulates the flow of water downstream. Many dams also generate electricity. Dams prevent flooding, but the reservoir behind the dam fills a valley that may once have been inhabited.

Diverting water into reservoirs protects houses on the flood plain

The sea wears down rock into beach pebbles and then sand grains

Large rocks, called rip-rap, are put in place to absorb the energy of waves, preventing the land from being washed away by the sea

A storm surge can flood the land

Groynes trap sand and gravel, protecting the beach from erosion

Sea defences

Storms at sea send huge waves crashing against the shore. Their power is immense. Coastal cliffs are the remains of hills, the rest of which have been washed away by the sea. It is not always possible to prevent the sea from eroding the coast, but some stretches can be protected. Sea walls (1) and loose rocks (2) absorb wave energy. Groynes (3) trap beach material. A closed barrage (4) will hold back a storm surge.

A dam prevents flooding downstream

Avalanche protection

Mountain communities know the slopes where the risk of avalanches is greatest. Barriers below the slope direct the moving snow away from homes, into areas where it does not pose a threat. The barriers also protect against hurricane-force winds that sometimes precede an avalanche.

Melting snow can make rivers overflow further downstream

An avalanche can move at up to 160 km/h

Drought protection

In areas where water is scarce, farmers practise 'dry farming'. Wild plants are allowed to grow in three years out of four, but from time to time they are lightly ploughed into the soil. By the fourth year the ground will be moist and fertile enough to grow a crop.

Avalanche barrier

Wildlife

Animals and plants have evolved ways to avoid extreme heat or cold. Desert plants store water in their leaves and stems, or grow only when it rains. Small rodents like the jerboa (*right*) spend most of the day in burrows, where it is cool. In cold climates some animals hibernate and sleep through the winter.

Excess river water can be used for irrigation

Tornado shelter

Renewable Energy

Renewable energy comes from natural sources that are replenished faster than they are used – for example, sunlight and wind. The Sun radiates a huge amount of energy. This energy produces our weather. It can also provide heating and be converted into electricity.

Some homes have water heaters on the roof. These collect solar energy, which is then used to heat water in a tank. Other buildings are equipped with solar panels that convert sunlight into electricity that can be used immediately, or stored in a battery to use later. Large solar ponds concentrate and store enough heat for use in industry. And if sunlight is focused on a large scale it can be used to run a solar power station (*right*).

Wind is caused by solar energy. It can also be used to generate electricity. Wind turbines are a familiar sight, but the energy from wind could be captured on a much larger scale.

Solar power station

An array of mirrors focuses the sunlight onto a furnace near the top of a tower. Sodium is heated in the furnace, and this is then used to convert water into steam, which drives a steam turbine.

Sunlight is concentrated and reflected towards the tower

A full-scale solar station can produce one tenth of the power of a large coal, gas, or nuclear power station

There are hundreds of panels, each with several mirrors focusing the sunlight

Solar generator

Hot sodium (**1**) passes through a heat exchanger (**2**) where it causes water to vaporise into steam. Once cooled (**3**), the sodium returns to the tower, where focused sunlight heats it again. Steam from the heat exchanger spins a turbine (**4**) to generate electricity. The steam then passes through a condenser (**5**) to be converted back into water before returning to the heat exchanger.

Solar farm

A solar farm works by using lots of solar panels that are grouped together in rows to capture sunlight and convert it into electricity. The electricity is then fed into a country's national supply for homes, hospitals, schools and businesses to use. Solar farms can be built on land that is not suitable for farming, but if they are built on farm land they can provide shade for crops and animals.

Wind power

Wind generators produce up to one million watts each, but only when the wind blows. The pitch of the blades adjusts automatically to suit wind conditions. The entire unit turns so the blades face the wind.

A motor rotates the unit to keep the blades facing the wind

The angle (pitch) of the blades is adjustable

Wind farms can be built on land (onshore) or in the sea (offshore)

Solar pond

Farms have windmills like this to pump water

Heat absorbed by solar collectors is transferred to the hot water tank

Solar ponds

In a solar pond, a layer of very salty water lies insulated beneath a layer of fresh water. The two do not mix because the salt water is much more dense. Black plastic covering the bottom of the pond absorbs solar heat, heating the salt water almost to boiling point. The hot water is then used to generate electricity.

Landscapes

Water seeps into tiny cracks in a rock. In winter, that water freezes. As it freezes, it expands, widening the cracks. When the ice melts in spring, the cracks are bigger. This happens every winter until the rock splits. Falling rocks crash into other rocks, breaking chips off them. Some of these fall into a river, where the flowing water rolls and grinds them together. Winds hurl other rock fragments into solid rock. Over thousands of years, they wear away. This process is called erosion.

Wind and water are continuously reshaping the landscape in this way. Sometimes, changes happen suddenly, such as in a big landslide or rockfall. But changes usually happen over thousands of years. Movements of the Earth's crust raise mountains. The weather then wears them down until they are smooth, rolling hills. Eventually, there is only a level plain.

Desert landscape

Wind and occasional rain producing torrents of water shape the desert surface. They wear rocks down to particles the size of sand and dust grains, then hurl these grains with great force against bigger rocks. The softer parts of the rock wear away first, leaving harder rock behind. These often form strange shapes. The loose sand is blown into dunes. The shape of dunes indicates the main wind direction.

Deep canyons are cut by rivers entering from outside the desert

A flat-topped hill or small plateau like this is called a mesa

A lake fills a hollow made by

Jagged mountains are young – in time, exposure to the weather will wear them smooth

Temperate landscape

Ice sheets, or glaciers, thousands of metres thick, have covered much of northern Europe and North America several times over the last two million years. The immense weight of the ice makes it flow and, as it moves, it scours away all the soil and loose rock. When at last the ice melts, the landscape is bare. But the area is marked with U-shaped valleys made by glaciers. These hollows that once held ice now contain lakes and piles of rocks, called moraines, that glaciers pushed into their present positions.

A small river runs through a large U-shaped valley that was made by a glacier

A hanging valley, made by a tributary glacier, ends with a waterfall

This beach was made when the sea level was higher

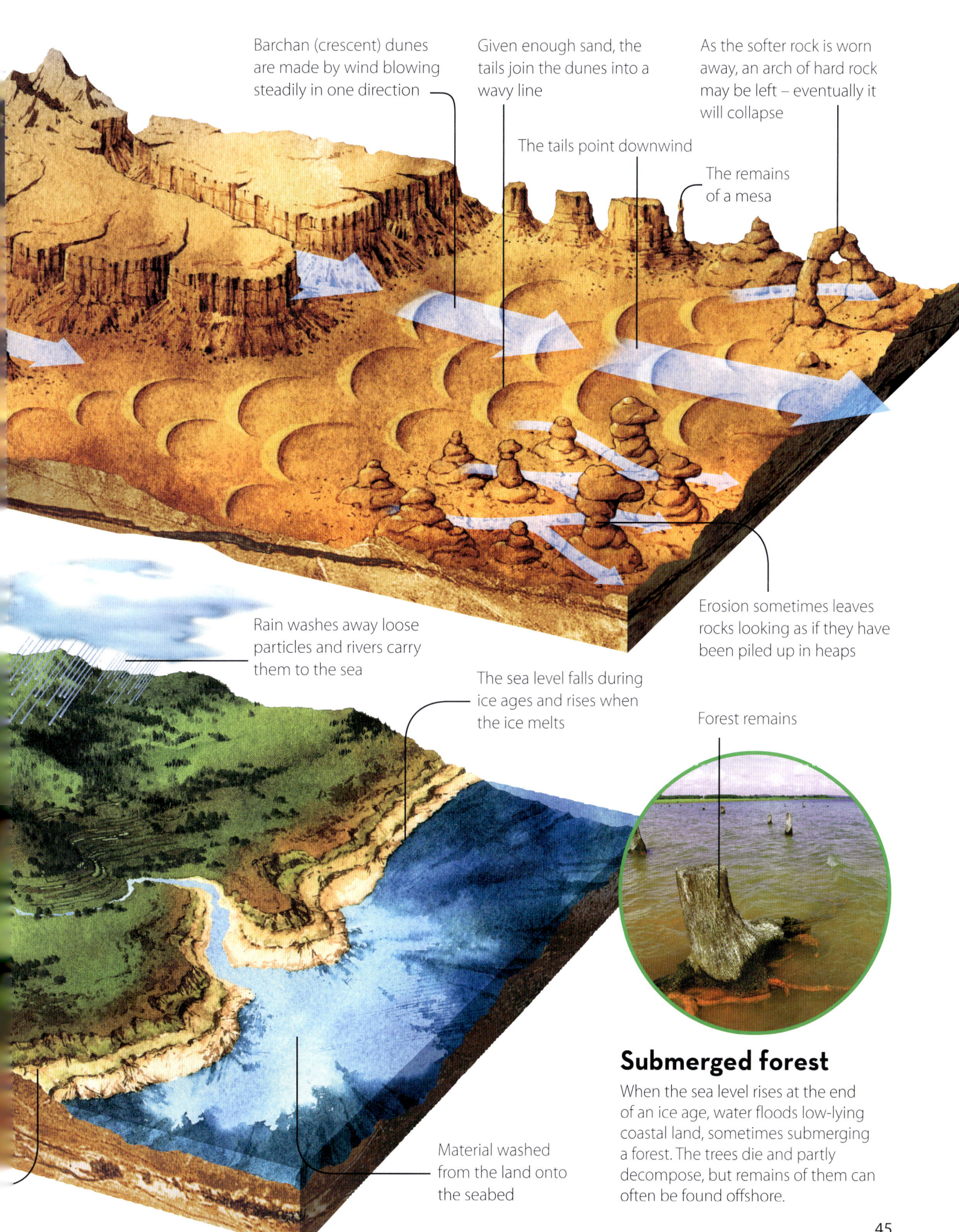

Submerged forest

When the sea level rises at the end of an ice age, water floods low-lying coastal land, sometimes submerging a forest. The trees die and partly decompose, but remains of them can often be found offshore.

Index

A
acid rain 36
air 6, 7, 10, 14, 16–26, 28, 34, 36
air pressure 16, 31, 34, 35
Antarctica 10, 11, 38
anticyclones 16
Arctic 10
atmosphere 6, 7, 30
aurorae 6
avalanches 41

B
Beaufort wind scale 30
breezes 11

C
canyons 44
cells 10, 11
climate 8–9
climate change 38
clouds 6, 10, 12–15, 17–27, 30, 34, 35, 38, 39
condensation 12, 14, 15, 17, 18, 20, 21, 24, 27
continental grasslands 8
continents 8
convection 14
cooling towers 15, 37
cyclones 17

D
dams 40, 41
depressions 16, 17, 19, 35
desert 8, 9, 11, 44
dew 12
dewpoint 31
drizzle 15, 17, 18, 20
drought 29, 40, 41
dunes 44, 45

E
Earth 6, 7, 10, 12, 16, 17, 32, 44
El Niño 29
Equator 10, 17, 20, 24, 33
erosion 40, 45
evaporation 12

F
factories 38
Ferrel cell 10
floods 29, 39, 40, 41, 45
fog 12, 37
forecasts 34–35
forests 6, 39, 45
freezing rain 21
fronts 16, 17, 18–19, 34

G
geostationary orbit 32, 33
glaciers 44
global warming 38–39
greenhouse gases 38–39
ground water 13
groynes 40
gyre 28

H
Hadley cell 10
hail 12, 20, 26
high pressure 16, 17, 34
highland climate 8, 9
humidity 30, 31
hurricanes 24–25, 29, 40
hybrid cars 36
hydrogen 12, 13

I
ice 8, 13, 14, 15, 20–23, 32, 35, 44, 45
ice ages 45
isobars 16, 34

J
jet streams 10, 11, 16, 17

L
La Niña 28
lakes 12–13, 44
lightning 22–23
low pressure 16–19, 27, 34, 43

M
magnetism 6
mammatus 27
mares' tails 19, 30
measuring instruments 30–31
mesa 44, 45
mesosphere 7
Meteosat 32, 33
methane 39
monsoons 29
moraines 44
mountains 13, 14, 15, 44

N
nitrogen 6
North Pole 6, 8, 10
Northern Hemisphere 7, 10–11, 16, 17, 28

O
occlusion 18–19
oceans 24, 28
orographic lifting 14
oxygen 6–7, 12–13
ozone 6–7
ozone layer 7, 38

P
Pampas 8
polar cells 11
polar climates 8
polar orbit 33
pollution 36–37
power stations 37, 38, 42
prairies 8
protection 40–41

Q
quarry 8

R
radiation 6–7, 33, 38, 42
radiometer 32, 33
radiosonde 30
rain 8, 9, 12–15, 17–21, 24, 26, 30–31, 34, 39, 40, 45
rainbows 12
reservoirs 40
ridges 17
rip-rap 40
rivers 12–13, 40, 44–45

S
satellites 25, 32–33, 34
sea 6, 10–14, 24–25, 34–35, 40
sea defences 40
sea level 39, 44–45
seasons 7
showers 18, 20–21, 34
smog 37
snow 6, 12–15, 17, 18, 20–21, 26, 29, 35, 40–41
solar power 32, 42–43
South Pole 6, 10
Southern Hemisphere 10–11, 16–17, 28
space 7
steppe 8
Stevenson screen 35
storm surge 24, 40
storms 29, 40
stratopause 7
stratosphere 7
Sun 6–7, 10, 14, 31, 38, 42
sunlight 6, 37, 38, 42
sunshine 30–31, 34, 36, 42
synoptic charts 34

T
temperate climate 8–9
temperate landscape 44
thermosphere 7
thunderstorms 15, 22–23
tornado turbine 43
tornadoes 15, 26–27, 42–43
trade winds 10–11, 28
tropical forest 8–9
tropics 20
tropopause 7, 11, 19, 22
troposphere 7
troughs 17
turbulence 23

U
ultraviolet radiation 6–7, 38

V
valleys 44
vapour trails 15

W
water 12–13, 29, 40, 44
water vapour 12–13, 14, 18, 20–21, 22, 37
waterspouts 27
weather balloons 30–31, 35
weather buoys 34–35
weather charts 16, 19
weather station 30–31, 34–35
wildlife 41
wind 10–11, 24–25, 26, 28–32, 36, 40–44
wind power 42–43